JONATHAN OLIVARES
SELECTED WORKS

pH **powerHouse Books**

Brooklyn, NY

CONTENTS

3

You can learn a lot about Jonathan Olivares from the design of his website, jonathanolivares.com. It is built in a slide projector format that allows visitors to click through images of his projects (objects, exhibitions, publications), sources of inspiration, works in progress, and designs in use. The credits page lists nearly a dozen contributors, which doesn't include those he has collaborated with on the projects themselves. There is minimal expository text. Olivares admits that the website is not his primary sales tool; clients do not find him this way. Instead, it is a statement about how a contemporary design practice operates, with one foot grounded in history and the other stepping into the future.

Olivares was born in Boston in 1981 and studied industrial design at Pratt Institute in Brooklyn, New York, where he graduated in 2006. After a yearlong apprenticeship with the industrial designer Konstantin Grcic in Munich, he returned to Boston to found his own practice, which encompasses industrial, spatial, and communication design, as well as design publication and research. In 2012 he moved to Los Angeles at the encouragement of the legendary Southern California designer Don Chadwick, the creator, with Bill Stumpf, of the Aeron chair, among other designs. Chadwick emphasized LA's proximity to a wide array of industrial manufacturers and its culture of openness and risk-taking. Olivares also liked the smell of the air when he stepped off the plane at LAX, which overlooks the Pacific Ocean.

By coming to California, Olivares was following in the footsteps of many legendary designers–Kem Weber, Greta Magnusson Grossman, Charles and Ray Eames, to name just a few. He is aware of this history and keenly interested and deeply knowledgeable about his forebearers. When one visits his studio, Olivares repeatedly turns the conversation to his bookshelves. He reaches for a treasured volume on Isamu Noguchi's design for UNESCO's gardens in Paris, a rare book about Marco Zanuso by Gillo Dorfles, or his perennial favorite, Frank Gehry: New Bentwood Furniture Designs. For the Vitra Workspace, a new type of showroom on the company's campus in Basel, Olivares encourages lingering and learning as much as purchasing by creating the Office Perspective, a thirty-one-foot-long illustrated chronology of the workplace. In the spirit of Charles and Ray Eames's information walls (most notably A Computer Perspective), the Office Perspective allows Vitra Workspace visitors to consider how their surroundings relate to this history, and perhaps even to envision the future of the office.

This book, which includes Olivares' realized projects and published writings, reflects the multivalent nature of his practice and encyclopedic knowledge of design. In "Sequence," he explores three design projects from the 1960s and 1970s that were associated with faculty or alumni of Harvard Graduate School of Design. Olivares draws connections between these seemingly unrelated plans and distills their similarities, recognizing that each sought to use design to improve everyday life and catalyze positive change in their communities. His books, A Taxonomy of Office Chairs, and Richard Sapper Edited by Jonathan Olivares, reveal his tenacity in fully exploring all sides of a complex subject, thus enriching his own work in the process.

For Olivares, writing influences design influences writing. Just two years after receiving his degree from Pratt, Domus magazine invited him to write a comprehensive review of American furniture manufacturing, "The US Furniture Industry." By conducting more than twenty interviews with furniture companies large and small, he became acquainted with many important figures, including Benjamin Pardo, Knoll's director of design. Pardo invited him to create the Olivares Aluminum Chair (2012), a lightweight indoor/outdoor stacking chair. The key to its functionality is a system of two nylon rails inconspicuously placed underneath the seat, which allow easy stacking and prevent scratching. Olivares's teenage hobby was skateboarding, and that feature was inspired by the nylon rails on 1980s skateboards that protect the image on the bottom of the board. In 2014 for the exhibition Source Material, co-curated with Jasper Morrison and Marco Velardi, Olivares chose the skateboard rail as his "reference object," explaining in the catalog that "these plastic rails are some of the first things I remember assembling as a young boy. . . putting a skateboard together was a terribly exciting affair because there was so much potential in it."

The Source Material exhibition epitomizes Olivares's collaborative method. While design is intrinsically collaborative, Olivares seeks out these opportunities, believing that they result in a better product and, possibly, a new paradigm for working.

For the Vitra Workspace, he partnered with the London-based Swedish architect Pernilla Ohrstedt to conceive the spatial arrangement, the furnishings, and the editorial content of the Office Perspective.

For the House for a Daybed installation at the 2016 Biennale Interieur in Kortrijk, Belgium, he worked with the Los Angeles architecture firm Johnston Marklee to create a captivating environment for his all-fabric furniture for the Danish textile manufacturer Kvadrat. Even on the Aluminum Bench created for Zahner in 2015, a project for which he received sole design credit, Olivares invited the artist Nate Antolik to create a series of drawings that imagined an alphabet of possible bench shapes. These were exhibited at the bench's first public showing at Volume Gallery in Chicago.

Like any designer, Olivares is concerned with making outstanding products, but that is not his sole aim. By strategically undertaking research projects that inform his own designs, pursuing collaborations with the potential for innovative breakthroughs, and taking risks with new partners, manufacturers, and modes of distribution, he is constantly questioning and redefining how a designer works in the twenty-first century.

SELECTED WORKS

THE US FURNITURE INDUSTRY

Today there is a segment of the American furniture industry that is focused on producing exceptionally designed contemporary furniture manufactured with the latest technologies. In 1947 when George Nelson's article "The Furniture Industry" was published in Fortune magazine, "Modern furniture of top design quality" was difficult to find in the United States. In the last sixty years a number of companies have come to comprise what we can call the US Furniture Design Industry. The largest of these companies employ thousands of people, while the midsized may operate with hundreds, and the smallest with as few as four. Although all manufacture in the US, some use a single factory, others rely on a global supply chain, and the largest operate regional factories in Asia, Europe, and North America. The market for this furniture is comprised of an increasing number of design-conscious architects, interior designers, showrooms, retailers, and individuals whose constant desire for new products creates a demand that furniture companies must satisfy. The entire industry is transforming as it deals with environmental issues. Quality of design depends on the vision and clarity of those who are responsible for it and varies from company to company. In 2006, 23,177 people attended the International Contemporary Furniture Fair in New York City, where attendance has more than doubled since 1996. Bravo and the USA network, two major American television channels, have created whole series on the subject of design. Increased American interest in design has created an exciting climate, new opportunities, and according to Alan Heller, founder of the New York-based furniture brand Heller, "a window open for design that we have not seen in America since the 1960s."

MANUFACTURING

Office furniture produced by American companies for the North American market is almost entirely made and assembled in the US. This furniture is all made to order, highly customized, and takes four to eight weeks to manufacture and deliver nationally. Speed and domestic production locations give American manufacturers of office furniture an advantage over their foreign competitors. Transportation by boat from China to the US takes four weeks and shipping within the US can take up to three, which puts Asian manufacturers of office furniture at a great disadvantage. According to Andy Geiger, Director of Case Good Manufacturing at Bernhardt Design, "Lean production models and new technologies allow customized furniture to be made at lightning speeds." Twenty years ago the lead-time for office furniture was between sixteen and twenty weeks. Today's improved lead times can be attributed to lean production methods, shortened delivery times from material vendors, computer programs such as Pro Engineer, and custom software that tracks and manages orders.

Bernhardt Design has three wood and upholstery factories in Lenoir, North Carolina.

Of twenty thousand components being manufactured on any given day at these factories, approximately eight thousand are customized in size and material for specific clients. Bernhardt's factories in Lenoir produce 70 percent of their furniture; the remainder is outsourced in China and North America. Herman Miller, a leading global provider of office furniture, has modeled their manufacturing after the Toyota Production System, sourcing components on a just-in-time basis from factories in China, Latin America, and North America. Steelcase, the largest manufacturer of office furniture in the US, supplies its furniture globally by operating regional production plants in Asia, Europe, and North America. Steelcase's furniture is produced in the region it will be sold in, so that products made in Asia, for example, are for the Asian Market.

Residential furniture is manufactured under its own constraints. It is sold through retailers, catalogs, and websites that often narrow choices to one size and a few color options. Typical lead time ranges from one day to four weeks. There is a considerable amount of crossover between what is sold for residences and what is sold for offices and commercial applications. Makers of residential furniture report that at least 50 percent of their products are sold to the commercial market. There is also a category of furniture, like Heller's seating and Knoll's Bertoia chairs, that is not specific to offices or residences but are sold for both.

Two prominent models for producing residential furniture exist. In the first, standardized furniture is produced and kept in inventory for fast delivery. This model limits the extent to which items can be customized but is ideal for high volumes. In the second model, lean production, inventory is considered wasteful and furniture is only produced once it is ordered. This allows a high level of customization and accommodates large orders. Customized furniture is often shipped directly from the factory to the customer.

Heller manufactures its furniture in volumes of ten thousand at third-party plastic factories in Italy and the US. By storing the furniture in warehouses in Missouri and Milan, Heller can guarantee delivery in as little as one day. Knoll, producer of office and residential furniture, makes Frank Gehry's Cross Check chair at a wood factory in North Carolina. An inventory of the chair is always kept to supply demand. Emeco, the aluminum furniture producer, makes 90 percent of its furniture for orders placed by retailers and specific commercial projects. The remaining 10 percent is made for inventory and is kept at Emeco's Hanover, Pennsylvania factory for anticipated orders. The Cherner Chair Company produces American architect Norman Cherner's wooden and steel furniture from the 1950s and 1960s as well as new designs by his son, and company cofounder, Ben Cherner. The chairs and tables are manufactured at US wood and steel factories for specific orders and shipped directly to customers, which eliminates the need for a warehouse. A retailer can order two Cherner chairs in cherry and another in maple and the factory will make them individually upon receipt of the order.

SALES

Sixty years ago retailers controlled the industry. Stores would remove brand labels from furniture once it arrived at their shops. Manufacturers made only what retailers knew they could sell, which was usually period furniture styled after the designs of the eighteenth century. Nelson commented: "The retailer is the man who stands between the progressive manufacturer and the public." Nelson however, noted exceptions: "the activities of stores like Bloomingdale's in promoting modern design sometimes take on even a crusading fervor." Since the 1940s however, the furniture design industry has cultivated its own network for distribution through showrooms, contract dealers, independent design retailers, and museum shops.

Most furniture is now sold through architects and interior designers who order furniture for the spaces they are designing. Independent and manufacturer showrooms help architects and designers throughout their design and installation process.

In the last decade, museum shops have become increasingly present in American cities, making design more accessible and increasing sales. The MoMA design stores in New York City have introduced the US to the Japanese design brand Muji, and stock a significant number of contemporary and classic twentieth century furniture designs. Enrico Bressan, co-founder of the Los Angeles-based home accessory company Artecnica, explained that, "There are good museum shops that are beginning to do business, not only in New York, Los Angeles, and Dallas, but also in Cincinnati, Ohio, Des Moines, Iowa, and Knoxville, Tennessee." Good shops have a profound influence on the market and design community.

During this decade, the most significant development in residential furniture sales has been the activity of retailer Design Within Reach. DWR is the first nationwide design retailer in the US and has sixty-three stores in twenty-four states. Their stores are located in heavily trafficked areas of cities, making them easily accessible to the public and creating a dialogue about design with Americans that previously did not exist.

THE ENVIRONMENT

Every company mentioned in this article has its own strategy for improving their environmental impact. Maharam, the US producer of textiles, stated in their "Approach to Environmental Marketing," that terms such as sustainable, green, biodegradable, and environmentally safe can be misleading and inaccurate. It is difficult to use such vague terms to describe the environmental activities that are taking place in the industry. What is certain is that the companies in this article are committed to efficient use of resources, the cleanest manufacturing possible, scientific material assessment, development of recycling and re-use programs, and improvement of human health for workers and customers. What is also certain is that the market is demanding cleaner standards and environmental information about products.

New criteria for environmental assessment is being defined by independent organizations such as the International Organization for Standardization. Such groups are working directly with the furniture industry to develop strategies that are specific to each company. In-house teams at the largest companies work to implement such strategies. Often small companies use fewer materials and production sources than large companies, which makes it less complicated for them to reach a high level of environmental sensitivity. There is much debate in the industry over which strategies for environmental manufacturing are best. However, competition between organizations inevitably produces varied and competitive approaches, which is good for the overall development of new standards.

DESIGN

For design to continue to define this segment of the furniture industry it must remain this segment's central activity. Despite the increasing complexity of the way that furniture is manufactured and distributed, designing remains a simple act. In response to the question, "Is the design process more complex today than it was in 1947?" Jack Tanis, fifty year veteran of the industry, former employee of Herman Miller, and current executive at Steelcase responded, "Good design today will anticipate needs rather than suit existing ones, and it was the same in 1947." However, the design process is

threatened by design briefs that start with a competitors existing product or rely too heavily on focus group opinion or consensus within a large group of executives. Nelson observed the danger of products based on public survey: "A product watered down to leave out everything people dislike inevitably ends up as a tasteless concoction with no positive qualities of any kind." The strongest design is still produced under the conditions described by Charles Eames's 1969 "What is Design" diagram, which shows the overlapping interests of the designer, the client, and society.

MOVING FORWARD

The Business and Institutional Furniture Manufacturer's Association (BIFMA) estimates that 2007 US consumption of office furniture will be $14.3 billion. However, sales alone do not guarantee design integrity. Whether design is a quality that the American public will continue to welcome or a passing buzzword that is serving marketing purposes is uncertain. To compete with increasing global competition, the US furniture design industry must achieve the highest level of sophistication in its planning, manufacturing, and design. Referring to the common acceptance of disposable products and obsolescence in the US Michael Maharam, Maharam's co-owner, stated: "The American production model is fundamentally unhealthy." Today responsibly-designed furniture must be heirloom quality, recyclable, or preferably both. As it may have been difficult for Nelson to imagine the current state of the furniture industry in 1947, it is difficult to predict where it will end up sixty years from now; the American market has a decision to make today. Will it embrace furniture that is intelligently designed and manufactured by those who believe in it or will it regard furniture as just another replaceable commodity?

THE US FURNITURE DESIGN INDUSTRY
DOMUS, MARCH 2007, PP. 104–9
This text investigated the state of the US furniture industry through visits to the major companies' headquarters and factories, and interviews with their leadership. Realized sixty years after George Nelson wrote an essay of the same title for Fortune magazine, this new article surveyed the industry's manufacturing, sales, environmental strategy, and design approach.

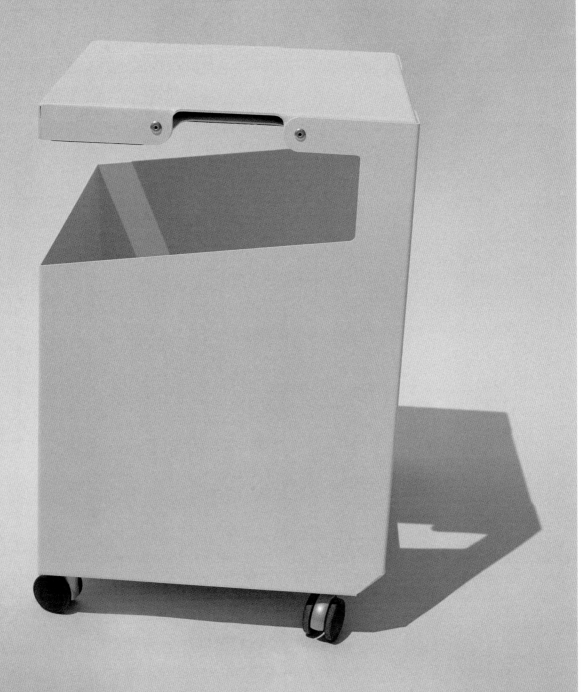

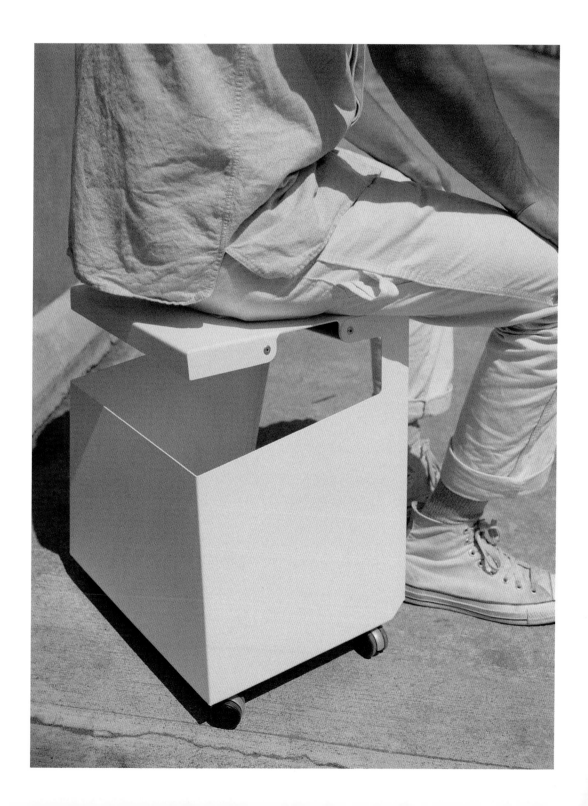

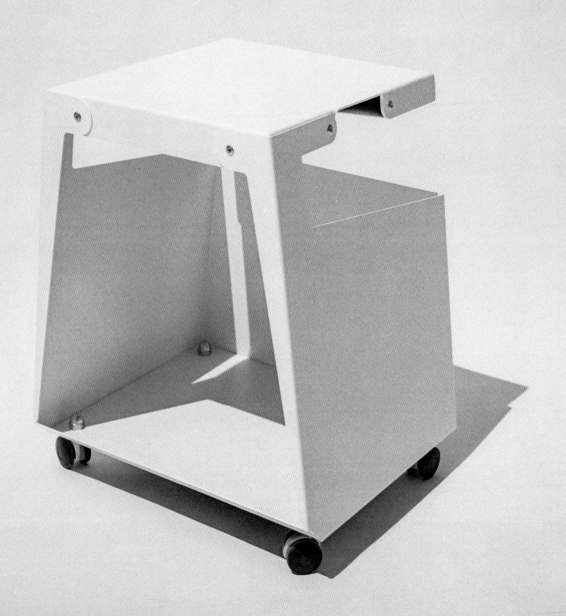

MULTI-PURPOSE STEEL CART (SMITH)
DANESE, ITALY, 2007
This cart was designed with the evolving needs of the
home in mind, allowing the stay-at-home worker to
temporarily convert a dining table into a desk by hanging
the cart from the table's edge. A contemporary toolbox,
the object is manufactured with laser-cut, folded, and
riveted sheet steel, and its construction was informed
by works designed using similar processes by Enzo Mari
and Bruno Munari for Danese throughout the previous
five decades. Part stool, part cart, part storage unit, part
side table, the object is ultimately defined by how its
owner puts it to use.

PUNK-CHAIRS

A stocky, Mexican, teenage rocker thrashes around the dance floor. In a tantrum, he kicks and punches, he's an indiscernible cluster of torn jeans, greasy black hair, flannel shirt, and creeper shoes. He barely avoids a collision with the only other guy dancing, a raging Texan: enormous, bald, twentysomething, in cowboy boots and overalls.

The band is playing next to them and the female lead singer is shouting, "I'm gonna burn, burn your house down!" Loud pulses of garage-punk emit from the band's mess of cables, angry faces, rigid arm movements, and sticker-covered instruments.

The thrashing on the dance floor grows more intense. The Mexican rocker spins out of control and knocks into a table, sending a glass ashtray shattering to the ground just next to the booth where Konstantin is seated. As he dances the Texan kicks over the microphone stand and it delivers a shriek of feedback. The Mexican picks up a sturdy wooden chair in his hands and shakes it violently, stomping the chair's legs on the floor in pace with the drums. He jumps, the chair falls, he kicks it, picks it up, and then he wipes out on the floor. Again, the Texan kicks the microphone stand–more loud feedback. The chair stands by itself and the Mexican is dancing wildly around it.

Konstantin and I exchange a glance but say nothing. We are both impressed with the energy, the chair, and the rockers. It continues. The Texan has now begun dancing with a different chair. Picking it up, he points its legs away from him like arms and together they push forwards and backwards.

The band leads one song straight into another, the dancing rockers and their chairs keep going and they all form a throng of loud, sweaty chaos. Dimly-lit pool table lights and a neon Budweiser sign cast their glow on a wall lined with full-scale posters of bikini calendar girls. I am attempting to make a movie with my camera, which I'll later realize is only capturing noise because Joe's Bar is so dark. Since the bar seems like it could easily host a bar fight, I'm careful not to point the camera for too long at the truck drivers playing pool or the locals seated at the bar. During this three day vacation in Texas we have observed that all bars have signs posted at their entrance forbidding firearms indoors, and this makes us slightly nervous. The band has stopped playing and is now packing up their gear. They announce that they are selling merchandise and Konstantin buys their CD. We learn that the punk band is called Sparkle Motion and are from Austin, Texas. Tired and satisfied, the Mexican sits on the chair. Unlike Le Corbusier's "human-limb-objects," which he describes as "docile," "discreet," and "self-effacing" servants to their human masters, the punk-chairs at Joe's bar have conspicuously strong personalities and through aggressive animation they become active characters.[1] I remember the lyrics of Elvis's Jailhouse Rock: "Don't you be no square, if you can't find a partner grab a wooden chair." It is clear that chairs still make good dancing partners.

1   LE CORBUSIER, L'ART DÉCORATIF D'AUJOURD'HUI (PARIS, 1925), PP. 76, 79.

PUNK CHAIRS
ABITARE, OCTOBER 2007, PP. 116–7
Written after a trip through western Texas and New
Mexico with Konstantin Grcic, this text recalls an
interaction we witnessed between a couple of punk
rockers and some objects in a bar. The notion that
objects are passive and docile things was called into
question as we saw that objects are just as much a part
of the animation of life as the people who use them.

THE EVOLUTION OF THE PORTALEDGE

Strange things happen under extreme circumstances. To satisfy the demands of bizarre conditions, furniture must abandon the assumptions that prevail in established designs. As climbers in the 1960s ascended new routes that required multiple days to climb, it became imperative for them to find ways to sleep on the rock wall. Drawing from hammocks, cots, tents, and sail construction, a generation of climber-designers invented a new typology: the portaledge.

1950s

Warren Harding slept on natural ledges during his first ascent of El Capitan in Yosemite in 1958.

1960s

The multiple day routes on El Capitan pushed climbers to invent structures for sleeping. They began securing traditional two-point hammocks to cliff walls. Warren Harding invented the first hammock suspended from a central point, which he called a BAT (Basically Absurd Technology) Tent. Central suspension facilitates deployment, prevents the tipping that occurs with two-point hammocks, and has since been integrated into every significant big wall sleeping structure. Harding almost died during his 1968 attempt on Half Dome in Yosemite after being trapped in a three-day storm, where his BAT Tent filled with freezing rain and snow. Single-point hammocks allowed little sleep because they offered no weather resistance and crushed climbers' shoulders.

1970s

During the early 1970s, climbers Billy Westbay and Bruce Hawkins created the first portaledges by appropriating steel and canvas cots stolen from park lodges in Yosemite. These were a vast improvement from single-point hammocks with regard to comfort, but they were not collapsible and weighed up to thirty kilograms (almost three times the weight of today's models). During this period climbers also used "submarine ledges," made from US Navy aluminum tube cots that had been purchased from army surplus stores.

In 1972, the climber brothers Gregg and Jeff Lowe designed the LURP, a highly innovative portaledge prototype. The design's collapsible frame allowed the Lowes to climb without the bulk of a cot. Every significant portaledge since the LURP has had a collapsible frame. Another pioneering feature of this design was its nylon fly tent, which provided an enclosed shelter from the elements. Fly tents quickly became a standard element of portaledges. Jeff Lowe used the LURP on the first winter ascent of Yosemite's Half Dome. Although the prototype was never sold to others, the brothers included it in their catalog of climbing products, which circulated widely among climbers.

By the late 1970s the term "portaledge," which combines the words "portable" and "ledge," had become the common name for the typology. The originator of the term remains unknown to this day. Mike Graham, a famous American climber, founded his climbing gear company Gramicci in 1977. Over the next five years, Graham sold over five hundred of the first commercially available portaledges, called Cliff Dwellings, to climbers in California and Europe. Graham made his Cliff Dwellings using equipment that he carried in his truck, and would set up his shop in friends' garages and basements. Graham's frame tubes slotted into each other at their corners, which allowed the frame to collapse into the smallest bag possible. His minimal corner connections were an important innovation, but they also made the Cliff Dwelling vulnerable to structural failure under extreme forces of nature. For an expedition to Patagonia in 1979 Graham designed the Fortress, the first portaledge large enough for two people. This model was constructed with ballistic nylon, a fabric strong enough to deflect small pieces of falling ice and rock. During the same year Graham made, but never tested, a prototype of a Windshield: a tent, suspended below the Cliff Dwelling that would deflect upward winds away from the portaledge.

1980s

Fieldware Designs, a climber-owned company, produced a chrome moly tube portaledge in 1986 that introduced separate 90° fittings as corner connections for the tube frame. These fittings solved the structural problems inherent in the Cliff Dwelling and have since become the standard connection for tube frames. Only a few of these designs were ever sold.

In 1986, the American climber John Middendorf founded A5 Adventures, a company specializing in portaledges and climbing bags, in Flagstaff, Arizona. With strengthened 90° corner fittings and thicker tubing, the A5 portaledge was structurally superior to any previous design. The A5 fly tent was made from a three ounce Oxford fabric with a heavy-duty waterproof urethane coating, which was fixed to the portaledge using draw cords that ran under the ledge. The fly's construction was inspired by tipi designs and folded out of a complex pattern with a single seam. This was a great advantage for waterproofing. The combination of these improved features made the A5 portaledge the first design capable of withstanding the world's worst storms.

1990s

With the advent of the portaledge, climbers began ascending big walls in Alpine style, which refers to a continuous ascent, with all of one's equipment. Prior to the portaledge, climbers had to climb in Siege style, securing hundreds of meters of rope along their entire route and setting up multiple camps along the way. Alpine style drastically reduces climbing time, which reduces the risk of encountering avalanches and blizzards.

In the decade following 1987, A5
sold over 2,200 portaledges, and the design
facilitated most ascents on extreme routes.
Middendorf's double portaledge introduced
"shark fin" fabric dividers between bed
areas, which serve as connection points
for three additional straps connecting the
central axis of the bed canopy to the central
suspension point. For the most extreme
conditions, A5 designed and produced a
Diamond Fly, which, as Graham's Wind Shield
prototype previously suggested, diverts
upward winds from hitting the underside
of the portaledge. During the 1990s, A5
was purchased by the California-based
outerwear company The North Face. The
new funding allowed Middendorf to enhance
his production process with the aid of
specialized outsourced tent production.

2000s

In 2001 Metolius, a climbing gear company
in Bend, Oregon began producing
portaledges and became the first major
competitor for A5. In 2002, A5 was
purchased by climber Conrad Anker, who
renamed the company ACE. Anker added
protective bumpers to the frame, integrated
pockets for drinks into the shark fins of
double portaledges and began anodizing the
aluminum tubing. Since 2005, Black Diamond,
a large mountaineering equipment company
based in Salt Lake City, has produced the A5/
ACE design in their factory in China.

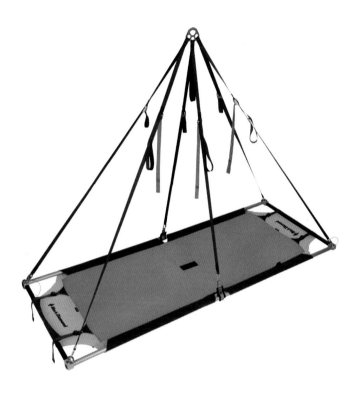

Single Portaledge, Black Diamond Equipment, USA, 2008

THE EVOLUTION OF THE PORTALEDGE
ABITARE, MARCH 2008, PP. 66–7

This timeline chronicles the development of the
Portaledge, the device used by climbers to establish
camp on vertical rock walls. The information was
compiled through interviews with the climber-designers
Conrad Anker, Mike Graham, and John Middendorf,
and formed the most complete history of this furniture
archetype assembled to date.

POLYURETHANE SEATING PLATFORM (TERRITORIO)
DANESE, ITALY, 2008
A study in the proportional limits of what constitutes
a chair, this seating platform allows a single person to
take a temporary rest with his or her belongings—bag,
phone, coffee—at their side. The semicircular form is
based on the reach of a seated person's arms, and the
soft polyurethane cushion provides a surprising degree
of comfort and the ability to drop one's things on it
without any noise or damaging impact. Designed while
I was writing "Evolution of the Portaledge" [P. 24], this
object demonstrates how a platform can provide a good
temporary resting place within an active environment.

PRODUCTS

Last June I attended a plastics trade fair in Chicago. Walking through a stadium-sized hall filled with the wares of mold manufacturers, I became lost in a maze of production tools and, as a result, it took me two hours to find the plastics companies I had come there to see. In a second hall I found hundreds of booths selling a host of bizarre metal gadgets and tubes, which I learned are the components that make the molds themselves. Many of today's products are created with the help of hundreds of other interdependent manufacturing products. I left the fair with the dizzying realization that the metal-gadget industry is built around the mold industry, which is built around the plastics industry, which is built around other industries like the automotive or furniture industry, which are built around real people's needs.

Products furnish our existence. They are all around us and appear in an incomprehensibly large variety. A world population of 6.7 billion, which data suggests will increase by almost 40 percent by 2050, assures that the gamut of human needs is wider today than it has ever been and is growing fast. Assuming that even the poorest of the world's citizens use a dozen products to execute their daily tasks, and factoring this into the global population, there's a staggering minimum of 80 billion products operating in today's society.

Merriam-Webster defines a product as: "Anything produced or obtained as a result of some operation or work, as by generation, growth, labor, study, or skill." Our society expands the definition by requiring that a product sell at some profit. Outside of these loose parameters, a clear expression of what products mean in the world today is surprisingly difficult to find. Encyclopedia Britannica, for instance, offers no entry on the subject.

In the everyday, products seem simple: we buy them, they serve a purpose, and if they cease to be useful, we discard them. A deeper look at the situation takes us down a rabbit hole where billions of inter-dependent products, hyper-specialized factories, massive shipping movements, a splintered design profession, and fanatical consumers obscure any unified sense of what products are, and lead us to numerous contradictions and questions.

The truth is, most of us live a life surrounded by products without the slightest clue as to where or how they're made—and for good reason. For instance, while shopping at a clothing store, little evidence suggests that entire industries are at work to make even the simplest items. Nothing there will tell you that your shoes were the work of professional manufacturers, designers, engineers, product developers, sales teams, marketing teams, accountants, lawyers, factory workers, shipping and receiving staff. And why should it? Most retail shops are in the business of selling products, not educating the consumer.

As we look around, it's easy to see that everything in our built environment is also constructed with products. Works of architecture are massive agglomerates of commodities churned out by the building industry: glass panels, beam fittings, ceiling tiles, carpeting, overhead lighting, HVAC systems, electrical conduits—the list goes on and on. What we don't see from the average building facade is that behind the scenes these products are rigorously assessed to meet the highest safety standards. It's not uncommon for facades to be built and tested at explosives facilities before they're realized in cities. Why? Car bombs. What does this mean? It means that windows are designed as much against explosives as they are for people, and of course, behind this act of bomb-proofing are more specialized products.

Transporting these things from their factories to their destinations is a shipping operation of massive scale and the largest of its kind in human history. Visualizing this phenomenon takes only an application of basic geometry to the dry financial figures we read in newspapers. Consider the fact that every year China exports $1.3 billion worth of car tires to the US, which sell at an average price of forty dollars. Unit cost over total sales tells us that in this particular business deal there are 32.5 million tires shipped across the Pacific Ocean. Given that the average car tire takes up .07 cubic meters, we know that these yearly shipments carry 2.2 million cubic meters of tire—which is more than double the volume of the Empire State Building. At this rate it would only take a decade to outfit midtown Manhattan with a rubber skyline. How do we accomplish such incredible shipments? It's done with the aid of thousands of other products like turbofans, shipping container cranes, and navigation software.

Shipping containers in particular have had a profound impact on how products are designed. The more compactly products fit inside a container, the cheaper the shipping cost per unit becomes. In home furnishings, Ikea is the master of this technique. A colleague of mine designed a bed system for the Swedish brand some years ago and the project was cancelled when it became apparent that the design was poorly shaped to meet the minimum quantity per container. Under these constraints, home furnishings have as much to do with the companies that transport them as they do with the places to which they are shipped.

The tendency with all these things is that products are increasingly designed around other products—metal gadgets for molds, windows for bombs, and furniture for shipping containers—and decreasingly designed around people. Another example of this is how competition in developed industries creates a flood of similar but different products. In this case the principle objective of the design is to stand out among others like it. As a result, every type of product generally comes in endless variations. This is conspicuously apparent in the bottled water section of any market, and here too, the bottles seem to speak more to each other than they do to us.

As consumers we have been conditioned to expect and accept products that look and function differently from precedent models. Change is a pillar of industry, and the technology and design professions are based on the belief that positive progress can be created through invention and improvement upon what already exists. An example of this is how typewriters were outdone by word processors, which in turn were superseded by computers. The basic function in each case–writing–is unchanged, but the level of performance is increased drastically with each successive model. For millennia, writing was achieved with pen and ink, but in the last century we have changed our facilities for this activity several times. Such shifts impact our behavior and our society profoundly. A small effect would be that children spend their time learning keyboards instead of cursive script; a large one would be that global communication is transformed forever.

Considering the immense power that products have on the social and political functions of our society, it's surprising that they go largely unchecked by government and institutions. Deregulated manufacturers can pretty much make and sell *anything*, as long as it doesn't result in injury, death, or a lawsuit. Ultimately the only real check and balance on products is the market, which leaves all the responsibility over much of our surrounding environment to manufacturers and designers.

When a politician does something even slightly scandalous, journalists are up in arms for weeks, but before a peep is heard from the press about a faulty product it has to go as far as severely injuring people–the toxic Mattel toys come to mind. The lack of criticism is understandable given that horrible designs are far less interesting and far more abundant than corrupt politicians. The few design critics there are justifiably spend their time writing about the products that inspire them over the ones that don't. However, a broad and deep reflection on products is lost amidst a total division between the politics, science, technology, and style sections of our newspapers. Under the jurisdiction of the style section, which largely functions as a trend-spotting shopping guide, the meaning of design is mostly conveyed through tasteful home furnishings, accessories, graphics, and fashion, and rarely through hard facts and larger social phenomena. The result is a misguided public that associates design exclusively with rarified products, and lacks the vocabulary to assess designs that carry heavier political impact, such as solar panels, subway cars, and medical equipment.

Humans have successfully cataloged most known plants and animals, yet any hope of doing the same for products was buried in landfills a long time ago. This hampers serious study on the subject, because we have few outstanding historical resources on which to base such an endeavor. The closest things we have to taxonomies of everyday products are vintage Sears Roebuck catalogs, and those went extinct years ago. Technical manuals for engine components are easy enough to come by, but the Library of Congress doesn't hold on to these things. In short, we have a better understanding of the natural world than we do of the one we have constructed, though whether we like it or not, the latter makes up our predominant reality.

If we turn to design museums for in-depth knowledge, we find that their collections focus only on the most inspired products, which collectively offer us a distorted bigger picture. The products that most profoundly affect society are not necessarily well designed. With few exceptions, design museums are little more informative than good retail shops. Both tend to be filled with perfectly nice products, but lack the depth of information that would give the public a greater sense of what objects mean in today's culture. Outside the institution, the general lack of information is only obscured further by the marketing profession, whose job it is to distract us from anything but satisfaction. You would have better luck getting free products from a company than unbiased information from its public relations team.

The values that our society places on products become clear when we look at the designers who garner the most attention. Lots of people know who Karl Lagerfeld is, fewer know what Philippe Starck does, fewer still know that Chris Bangle designs automobiles, and almost no one could name the best wind turbine designer. While we tend to like, understand, and appreciate simple products, we are not easily enamored with technical or infrastructural things. This has as much to do with how products are marketed and covered in the media as it does with the public's ignorance regarding engineering and technology. And the two only perpetuate each other. No one gets excited about buying a new car battery, but a new lounge chair is a different story.

As a result, there are countless coffee table books on chair design and few good resources on the infrastructural products that distinguish our time from the twenty-first century BC.

One would think that the industrial design field might at least have developed some internal solidarity on how to go about making a product, but there's as little consensus there as anywhere else. The profession is barely a hundred years old, but since its beginning, ideological differences have caused division, argument, fragmentation, and specialization.

In the early twentieth century, while a craft-based decorative approach caved under rational functionalism in Europe, a modern decorative movement gave way to streamlined styling in the US. Exiled by Nazis, the proponents of functionalism immigrated to the States, where some Americans were developing a functional organic design. To cater to the specialized needs of the postwar automotive industry, automotive design schools formed independently of industrial design schools, creating an academic and vocational division that still exists today. The field was further segregated, as some corporations created in-house design teams and ceased to rely on independent design offices. While streamlined styling diluted into lesser forms of styling, functionalism flourished, turned into clean-cut modernism, and eventually won people's favor. Then boredom set in, which was followed by disbelief in commercialism, anti-design, ergonomics, and a growing distrust between the in-house and independent designers. With postmodernism came more arguments. Out of frustration, some designers succeeded into a new profession where they could be taken seriously, at least briefly: product design. Since then, the field has disbanded into nothing less than anarchy.

In an essay expressing frustration with this phenomenon, the American designers Bruce and Stephanie Tharp list the plethora of specialized methods from which today's designers can choose: "user-centered design, eco design, design for the other 90 percent, universal design, sustainable design, interrogative design, task-centered design, reflective design, design for well-being, critical design, speculative design, speculative redesign, emotional design, socially responsible design, green design, conceptual design, concept design, slow design, dissident design, inclusive design, radical design, design for need, environmental design, contextual design, and transformative design." [1]

They missed a few, but the list is still telling. The absence of a philosophical unity in the way we go about making things is a symptom of our technologically driven, globalized culture. From the Bronze Age until very recently, individual cultures had their own specific ways of making objects, but today there are as many ways to make products as there are designers and manufacturers.

Currently, artists are the only group with the clairvoyance to shed light on some of the larger phenomena surrounding products. More than any other sources,

Andreas Gursky's photos of factory workers, Damian Ortega's Cosmic Thing, and Edward Burtynsky's Manufactured Landscapes give us a vivid understanding of who makes products, how they are built, and what effect they are having on the environment. Why this should be has as much to do with our distance from these happenings as it does with the artist's ability to convey them. In simpler times, people knew the craftsman who made their goods, understood the basic tools used to make them, and lived in odorous proximity to where they were dumped after use.

The segmentation of today's consumer, retailer, manufacturer, and waste system leaves each with little knowledge of, or impact on, how the other functions. Uninformed sales staff have never seen a factory floor, and therefore can't possibly explain its workings to the customer. What few factories are open to the public are not exactly destinations for tourists and school groups. Consequently, the public has no way of distinguishing what has been made on an eighteen-hour shift, in a poorly ventilated factory—by underpaid, underage workers—from what has been made in positive working conditions.

Market studies, focus groups, and intuition combined can't predict how the public will respond to a product once it's released. Don Chadwick, the American

1   BRUCE THARP AND STEPHANIE THARP, "DISCURSIVE DESIGN," INDUSTRIAL DESIGN SOCIETY OF AMERICA (VIRGINIA, 2008), PP. 237–45.

designer, once explained to me that when he, Bill Stumpf, and Herman Miller took a leap of faith with the Aeron chair, none of them had a clue that the design would result in what is now *the* ubiquitous office chair. And how could they have known how millions of people would react to their product before they started selling it?

The geographical gap that separates consumers, manufacturers, and the waste we all create is perhaps the bleakest of all. A few examples are enough to depict the grim reality. The Great Pacific Garbage Patch is an island in the Pacific Ocean twice the size of Texas and made up of discarded plastic products carried and trapped by ocean currents. Western countries dump mountains of old products on poor countries willing to sell landfill space. Cities of e-waste have popped up in Africa and Asia, where local inhabitants sift through toxic heaps of old keyboards, computers, and monitors, salvaging parts for profit while poisoning their communities.

Nevertheless, our faith in products is unwavering. Like sports teams, religion, and TV, products gather large groups of devoted followers. Days before a new iPhone is released, eager customers equipped with tents and camping chairs begin queuing up outside Apple stores. In 2008, the opening of the Harajuku H&M shop drew approximately 2,500 fashionistas, who waited in line for hours in the cold November rain to be the first ones in. Amidst a vast abundance of products, our obsession with them leads us to behave as though they were in short supply.

Some recent tendencies in technology and design are pointing towards a conceivable decline in tangible products. Software, digital information, and communication are all achieved with little in the realm of physical material. The letter openers, paper trays, calculators, calendars, Rolodexes, and landline telephones that characterized my mother's desk are not on mine—they're in my pocket. Single digital products are eliminating entire series of disparate objects.

Another interesting shift away from physical products is in the focus given by some in the design industry to designing services and activities geared towards improving customer service strategies and corporate work patterns. The fact that both the clients and the design consultancies are speaking of design in terms of *service* and not *product* implies a world with fewer products and more activities. This would do wonders for the obese children who never get outside. Yet until products become invisible, we're still left with billions of them to figure out what to do with.

The more products our culture turns out, the more contradictions appear around them. We can equate the widening gamut of products with an increase in their specificity to each other, and a decrease in their relationship to us. Boosted unit sales mean boosted unfamiliarity between the manufacturers and their customers. The more industry and manufacturing grow, the farther they get from our doorsteps and the less we understand their processes.

The same can be said for garbage. It's ironic that we are trashing the natural world, which we cherish, admire, and study, for products that we don't care enough about to document. Surrounded by an abundance of products, we take desperate measures to acquire them. Our willingness to accept novel tools and rapidly change our behavior around them makes us the most adaptable civilization yet. Still, our astounding ignorance of how these tools are made, distributed, and disposed of makes us the most oblivious. While we have little control over the rate at which products are made, we do have the ability to control our knowledge and thus our interaction with them.

Even amidst the growing complexity that surrounds them, products maintain their power to imbue our lives with a sense of fulfillment. The best products are tools that enhance our lives, allow us to do things that would otherwise be impossible, and give us great pleasure. Think of the difficult work of street cleaners and the essential brooms that help them do it, or the excitement to be had with a wonderful fishing lure. Imagine the incredible satisfaction of eliminating electricity bills and pollution by installing a state-of-the-art wind turbine on your roof. Made with positive intentions, products like these aren't designed to dupe you, grab your attention over other items on the shelves, or end up floating in the ocean. The overwhelming challenges that stand between human needs and the products that answer them can only be solved optimistically if they are understood. With such knowledge and optimism, our chances for a healthy manufactured and natural world increase exponentially.

PRODUCTS
DESIGN REAL BY KONSTANTIN GRCIC
ED. JULIA PEYTON JONES, HANS ULRICH OBRIST
(LONDON: SERPENTINE GALLERY; KOENIG BOOKS, 2010)
PP. 9–19
Commissioned to accompany the catalog for the
exhibition Design Real, curated by Konstantin Grcic
for the Serpentine Gallery in London, this text explores
the complex meaning of products in our world.
From where and how products are made to the shipping
infrastructures that transport them, and from the
regulations around what can be sold as a product
to the scant consensus among designers about how
to make them, the essay sheds light on the larger
societal context that surrounds products today.

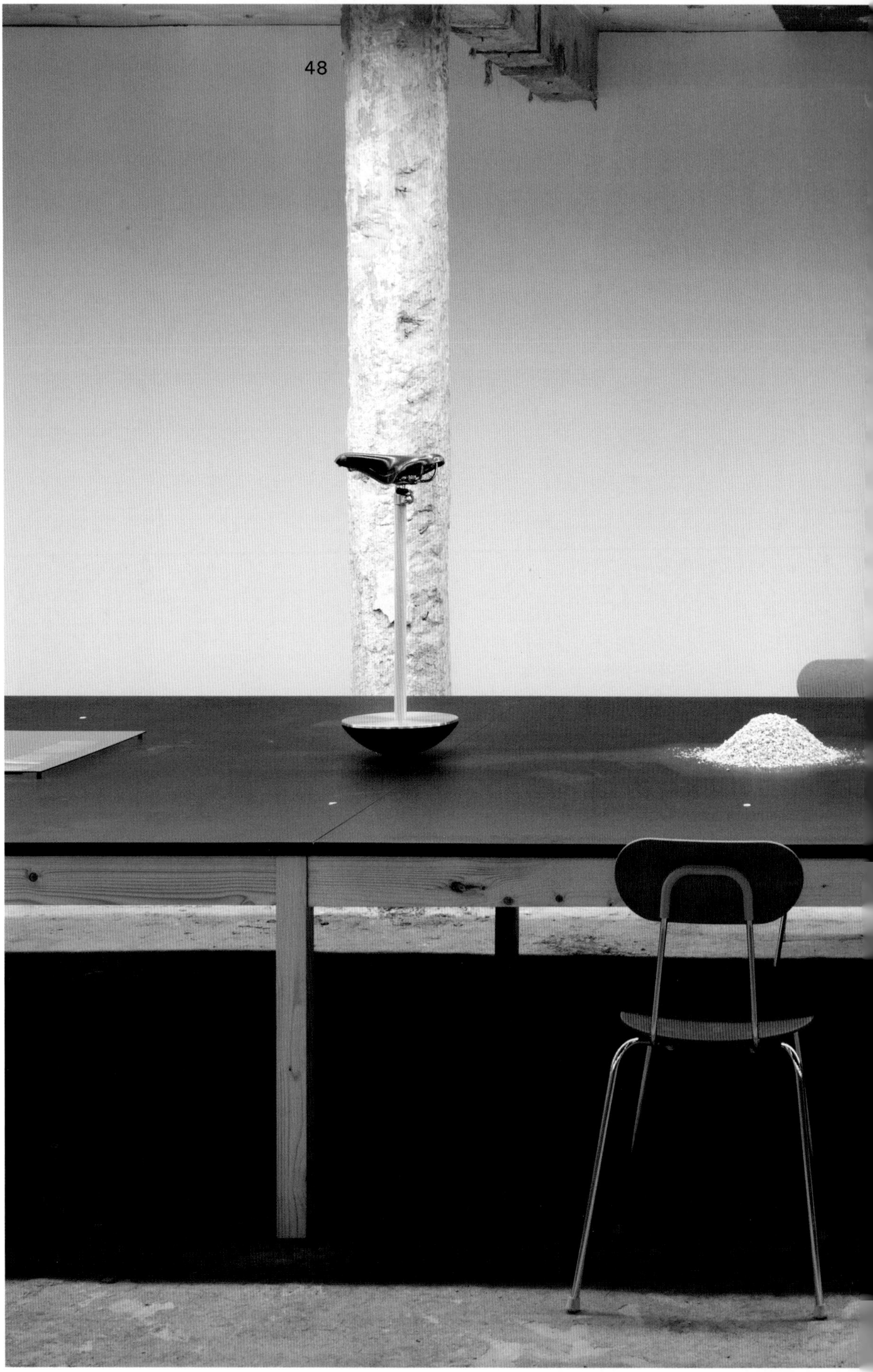

USELESS: AN EXPLODED VIEW
EXD BIENNALE, MUSEU DO DESIGN E DA MODA,
LISBON, OCTOBER 2, 2011–NOVEMBER 27, 2011
This exhibition was curated and designed for the
design biennial in Lisbon, which centered on the theme
of uselessness. Some thirty objects and films that
conveyed the multifarious definition of "useless" were
displayed on a 130-foot (40-meter) long table flanked by
chairs, an arrangement meant to encourage discussion
and engagement. Visitors could take a seat, study
the objects, watch the videos, and read an exhibition
pamphlet that provided additional information on each
of the items on display. The museum let us open the
windows onto the street below, which, in combination
with the sounds from the videos, created an acoustic
shelter that allowed visitors to have discussions within
the exhibition without disturbing other visitors.
The objects on display ranged from a barrel of oil
(barrels of oil are no longer used to transport oil) and a
pile of e-waste to objects of sport such as a skateboard.
The show ended with a rack of T–shirts in forty colors
and the exhibit pamphlet stated: "The world doesn't
need a T–shirt in every color of the rainbow–but it's
nice to have the option. Design is largely about the
subtle things in life, which contrary to popular belief,
aren't useless."

Contenu des iPads

1. Claude Rosticher du Groupe Signe anime l'atelier Montgolfière. On en suit les différentes étapes, jusqu'au lancer final « Le clair de lune » de Claude Debussy en fond sonore renforce le climat poétique de la manifestation.
2. Groupe Signe 2012 : interview des artistes à l'occasion de leur exposition au NMNM Villa Paloma. Quarante ans plus tard, les convictions restent intactes et les questions toujours d'actualité.
3. l'Œuvre du Mois : Simon Jacquard. « Les travaux de Simon Jacquard se propagent en combustion lente et à la vitesse d'un rêve d'escalier. Ses apparents dialogues de sourds n'excluent cependant jamais la référence aux matières premières du réel. » (Francis Mary)

On the iPads

1. Claude Rosticher of Groupe Signe runs the Montgolfière workshop, whose different stages can be followed up to the final throw, to the strains of Claude Debussy's Clair de Lune to enhance the event's poetic mood.
2. Groupe Signe 2012: artists' interview for their exhibition at NMNM Villa Paloma. Forty years later, the convictions are intact and the questions remain.
3. Work of the Month: Simon Jacquard. "Simon Jacquard's works spread like slow combustion with the speed of a spiral dream. Yet his seeming dialogues of the deaf never exclude a recurrent reference to the raw materials of reality." (Francis Mary)

Sull'iPad

1. Claude Rosticher del Groupe Signe anima il workshop Montgolfière. Ne seguiamo le diverse fasi, fino al lancio finale. "Il chiaro di luna" di Claude Debussy come colonna sonora rafforza il clima poetico della manifestazione.
2. Groupe Signe 2012: interviste degli artisti sulle loro mostra al NMNM Villa Paloma. Quarant'anni dopo le opinioni restano intatte e le domande rimangono.
3. l'Opera del mese : Simon Jacquard. "Il lavoro di Simon Jacquard si diffonde come una lenta combustione con la velocità di un sogno a spirale. Così i suoi apparenti dialoghi dei sordi non escludono mai continui referimenti alla materia prima della realtà." (Francis Mary)

Outils

La Table des Matières éveille vos sens et votre esprit critique. Elle est à la fois un lieu où se croisent différents chemins de connaissances et d'où partent de nouvelles pistes à explorer. Un atelier au sein duquel vous avez accès à une multitude de contenus et d'instruments pour comprendre, aimer et rêver le monde qui nous entoure. Des idées à noter? Un nom d'artiste à retenir? Une inspiration soudaine? Vous trouverez dans ces boîtes de quoi capturer quelques idées, griffonner, assembler, jouer, plier, colorer, recopier...

Tools

La Table des Matières hones your senses and critical capacity. It is both a crossroads for knowledge and a hub for new orientations to explore. It is a workshop that provides access to a wide range of content and tools to understand, love and envision the world around us. Have ideas to write down? Want to remember an artist? Have a sudden inspiration? These boxes provide what you need to jot down a few ideas, scribble, assemble, play, fold, colour, transcribe...

Strumenti

La Table des Matières risveglia i vostri sensi e il vostro spirito critico. È al contempo un luogo dove s'incrociano diversi cammini di conoscenza e da dove partono nuove piste da esplorare. Un laboratorio dove avrete accesso ad una moltitudine di contenuti e di strumenti per capire, amare e sognare il mondo che ci circonda. Delle idee da annotare ? Un nome d'artista da ricordare ? Un'ispirazione improvvisa ? In queste scatole troverete il necessario per afferrare idee, scarabocchiare, mettere insieme, giocare, piegare, colorare, ricopiare...

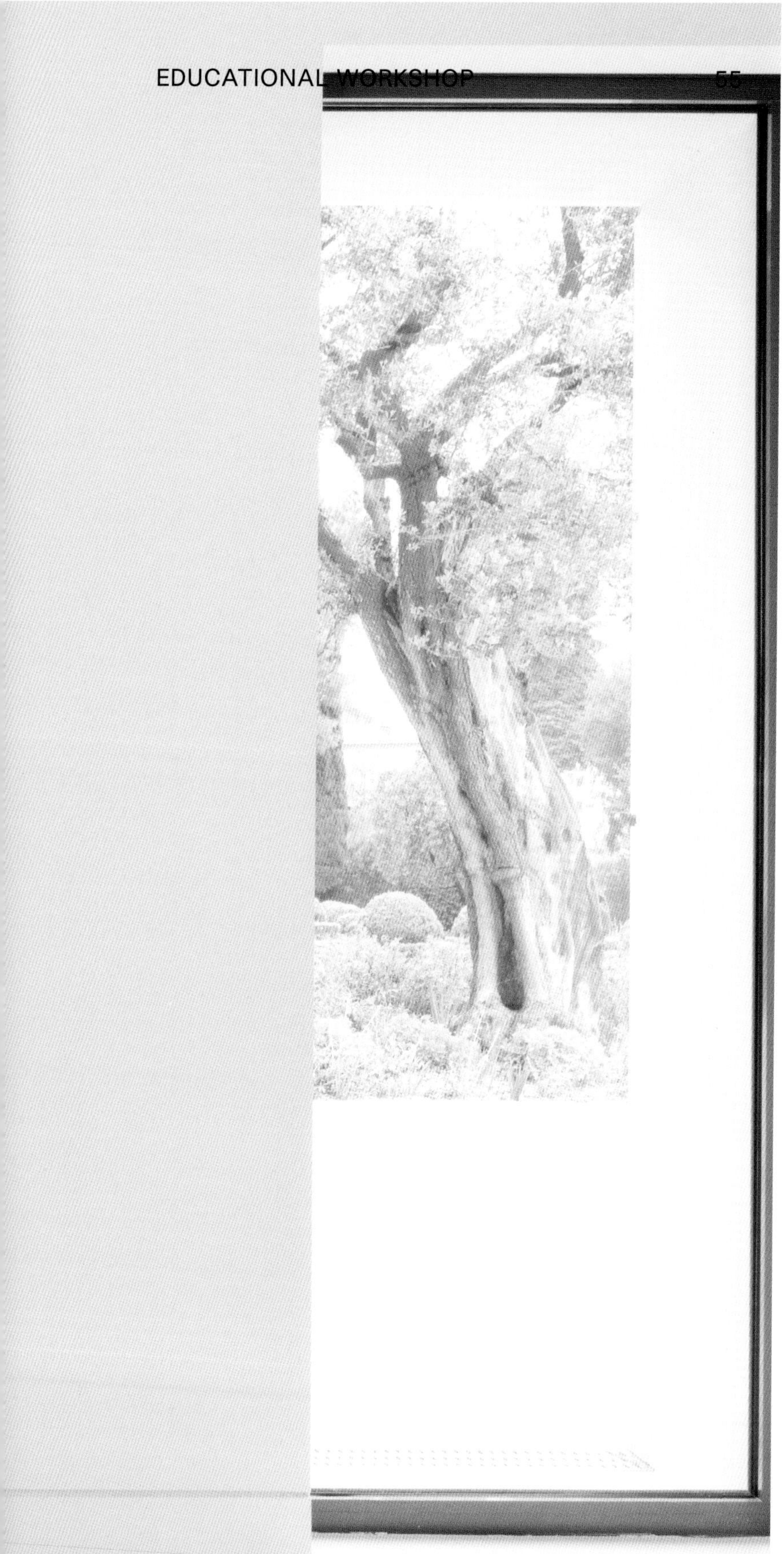

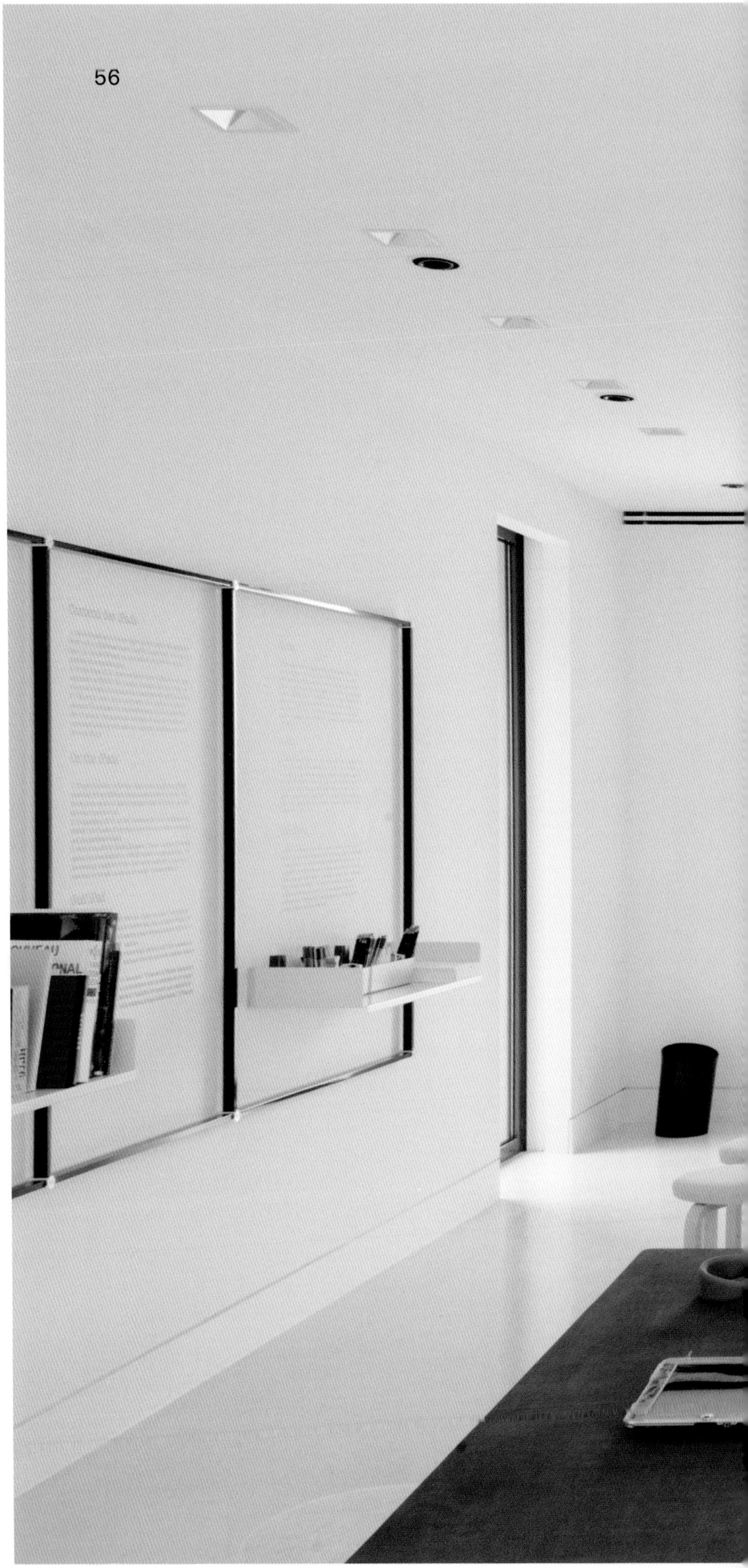

EDUCATIONAL WORKSHOP
(LA TABLE DES MATIÈRES)
NOUVEAU MUSÉE NATIONAL DE MONACO, 2012
Planned as an educational workshop, this space hosts
hundreds of Monégasque school children each year
for sessions with the museum's educational team,
and it provides regular museum visitors with a library
and a social hub where they can further their learning
about the museum and its current exhibition. The space
houses a variety of engaging materials used within the
workshops: a revolving library of books that focus on the
artists currently on view within the museum; plants from
the museum's garden, which are grown in collaboration
with municipal gardeners and a local restaurant;
art supplies; iPads with artist interviews; and a news
bulletin about local events. An aluminum scaffolding
frames the room's contents and provides a place for
trilingual descriptions that orient the self–guided visitor
in the space.

JONES

With the patent applications filed and the
bank loans pending approval, thirty-year-old
designer Jones, of Los Angeles, was on the
heels of success. Soon he could begin work
on his big idea: the world's first chair made
of thin air.

JONES
ULTRA JOURNAL, APRIL 2012, P. 5
For the Ultra Journal, a publication coinciding with the
release of the Ultra Chair by Clemens Weisshaar and
Reed Kram, the editors asked me to contribute a text in
the spirit of the Novels in Three Lines that the anarchist
and art critic Félix Fénéon published in the early
twentieth century. While Fénéon's Novels were bleak,
I decided to write a semi-autobiographical text that
celebrated the risk-taking, ambition, and blind optimism
that is required in the production of great design.

TODAY'S WALLS

Over the past five years, due to a breakup, a change of neighborhood, a search for a larger space, then an even larger space, and a move to a new city, I ended up moving apartments six times. All but the last move involved building or taking down an interior wall, so drywall, steel studs, and screws have been as much a part of the routine as U-Haul trucks, cardboard boxes, and packing tape. The actual building of a non-structural wall goes quickly, but the spackling, sanding and painting is the real time vacuum. At its best a wall of this sort blends in with the other walls, which are usually made of the same material, and helps them define a liveable volume, but the results are only as stunning as drywall and paint allow—which is to say, not so stunning.

The latest apartment I moved into is a design of Frank Gehry's (no DIY construction required) and the walls are also made of drywall. These walls are cleanly built and edged with wooden boards, but they aren't so different from the ones I built myself. There is something hugely disappointing about the realization that drywall, the default DIY solution, also happens to be the building industry's technique of choice.

Drywall is an invention of the early twentieth century, a paper-wrapped concoction of gypsum, starch, fiberglass, foaming agent, wax emulsion, and mildew-resistant additives. Because these materials are widely and cheaply available, when combined they pass the fire codes and building regulations, and the end product

requires little skill to install, drywall has become the standard wall-making product of our time. Just as the ancient Egyptians are remembered for their chiseled and monumental stone walls, and pre-industrial Japan had its beautifully-crafted and light-weight shoji screens, we will go down as the people that walled our homes with texture-less drywall.

The only time I have ever seen drywall look amazing is in the basement of SoHo's Prada store, where OMA left the green drywall and white spackle exposed. All of a sudden drywall was drywall, naked and proud of itself. One reason that drywall is so lame is that it was designed to hide behind paint and wallpaper. Even if the drywall companies would actually design the paper they use to wrap their gypsum concoctions, which would be unusually thoughtful, the assembly of it all lacks integrity. The spackle is there to obliterate any sign that the boards were ever assembled, the studs underneath the boards are crudely screwed together, and the whole structure is usually nail-gunned into the floor and ceiling. Another reason why drywall is so lame is that it allows contractors to hide all sorts of messy construction behind a seemingly clean surface.

What's so spectacular about the building techniques of times past is that they revealed their own construction: the Egyptian stones met each other on cut seams, the wooden and paper shoji was wonderfully jointed, and even plaster, the predecessor to drywall, left the texture and movements of whatever tool applied it. All of these details give the eye something pleasant to look at, whereas drywall gives nothing except the paint used to cover it.

Exterior walls don't face this dilemma; there are plenty of self-evident, cost-effective materials going up on the facades of buildings today. And anyone with a robust budget and a good idea can use any number of elegant materials suited for interior walls. The problem is that our default wall is a boring and soulless thing, and efficiency, economy, and standardization have come at the cost of texture, quality, and craftsmanship.

TODAY'S WALLS
APARTAMENTO, SPRING/SUMMER 2012, P. 10
As my interest in the built environment broadened from products to the spaces that contain them, I began to look critically at some of the uninspired building products that surround us. This text focuses on building walls, some inspired historical wall-building techniques, and the quality (or lack thereof) in the building industry's favorite wall-making product: drywall.

ALUMINUM CHAIR
KNOLL, USA, 2012
This die-cast aluminum stacking chair was the result
of research into aluminum forming and aluminum molding
techniques, exploring the limits of contour, weight,
and comfort within the material. Pushing the moldable
material thickness in die-cast aluminum to its minimum
allowed for a continuous contoured seating surface.
As a result of this breakthrough in manufacturing, the
chair could be dialed into a desired weight and offer
a level of seating comfort that far exceeds that of
the typical metal chair. To save weight, the legs are
manufactured as hollow extrusions, and it was decided
that these should be rectangular in order to limit the
soft shapes of the seat shell by encouraging a rectilinear
edge for the entire chair. The interplay of softness on
the seat surface and hard linearity at the chair's edges
provides a great deal of formal complexity.

SEQUENCE

An enticing request from the editors of this book to find historical links between the Graduate School of Design (GSD) and the field of Industrial Design has had me searching for works that were in one way or another connected to the School, its graduates, or its faculty. What surfaced was a cluster of disparate ventures from the 1960s and 1970s, by a group of designers who were part of the second generation of American modernists: a 1965 gas station program for Mobil Oil by Eliot Noyes who graduated from the GSD in 1938; the 1969 Design Research retail store by Benjamin Thompson, who served as the School's architecture department chairman from 1964 to 1968; and some since-proven hypotheses for reducing visual pollution and increasing quality of life in cities by George Nelson and the 1973 class he taught at the School.

The series of projects seemed random at first, but the more I looked at them, the clearer it became that they were united by more than the generational bond of their creators. These works laid the groundwork for aspects of everyday life that we now take for granted and used design as a vehicle for promoting positive social values. They encouraged respect for the individual, educated communities, and promoted physical enjoyment. Seen collectively, these three projects reveal that the winter of American modernism was in fact very warm.

Noyes's design program for Mobil Oil included graphics, industrial design, and architecture, and was intended to create a unified brand image that would help distinguish the company in the mind of the consumer. During initial research, Noyes discovered that Mobil stations were covered with advertisements from local purveyors of products and services, traversed by plastic pennant flags intended to draw attention to the stations, and painted with floor markings to direct traffic—all of which drew customer attention away from the primary reason for their visit, refueling. Even worse, many of the Mobil stations that Noyes first encountered lacked protective awnings to shield customers and employees from the elements.

Noyes hired Ivan Chermayeff and Tom Geismar to work with him on Mobil's logo and graphic system, and the group jettisoned the jumble they found and introduced clear signage to designate products and services. This alone would have simplified life for busy customers, but Noyes also introduced circular awnings above each gas pump, which blocked the sun and rain, and lit the gas pumps at night. From 1964 (the year Noyes was hired) to 1965 (the year that his solutions were implemented), millions of customers began experiencing a dramatic improvement in service in hundreds of communities with Mobil stations.

Four years after Noyes's gas stations were realized, the architect Benjamin Thompson moved his retail store Design Research (D/R) down the street from its original location in Harvard Square into a new building that he had designed to house the shop. Thompson's generation of architects faced the challenge of finding suitable furnishings for their modern interiors at a time when few commercial solutions existed. D/R had been set up in 1953 to address this problem.

By mixing products from different designers and manufacturers, Thompson created the first lifestyle shop, where customers could choose from a variety of options based on personal inclinations. The shop stocked furniture by Alvar Aalto, Marcel Breuer, Charles Eames, Joe Colombo, Vico Magistretti, and Hans Wegner, and a diverse array of kitchen, bath, and clothing products. Prior to D/R, consumers were limited to furniture manufacturers' showrooms, where they would find one designer's singular vision of what a home should look and feel like. The D/R customer wasn't only given more choice and freedom, but was included in and educated by the selection process, which was a form of design in itself. This retail strategy has since become commonplace, and the mixed approach has also been adopted by many of the best furniture manufacturers, who work with a roster of designers to offer furnishings that suit a wide range of personal styles.

Design Research was not only the first venue selling a plurality of design approaches under one roof, but also the store that most visibly did away with its walls. The D/R that opened its doors in 1969 was a five-story building with floor-to-ceiling glass panels placed between concrete floor slabs. The goods the shop sold were vividly colorful and displayed in dynamic arrangements throughout the floors, all of which were visible from the street. The

visual stimulation would have lent warmth to the neighborhood in a way that only the best bazaars do; even passersby would have shared in the excitement. A gesture like this shares design and the traits that are intrinsic to it—such as craftsmanship, logic, structure, form, and personality—with the community.

Yet not all buildings are as beautiful as D/R, and George Nelson sought solutions. In 1973 Nelson—architect, writer, and dominant figure in industrial design—led a group of GSD students through an exploratory project aimed at reducing visual pollution and increasing the quality of space in cities suffocated by an overabundance of buildings. The Hidden City, as the project was called, was based on some very simple ideas. Nelson hypothesized that if windowless buildings such as power stations, convention centers, and parking garages could be rebuilt as earth-covered mounds or placed underground, some spatial relief could be achieved in dense cities, providing room for public parks and dynamic pedestrian walkways.

The hypothesis was proposed through an essay written by Nelson, and a series of designs done by his students at the GSD. His essay he stated:
"These hypotheses indicate some possible physical improvements, but they are also symbols. As symbols they stand for the belief that vision, at this point in time, is more important than new technology, for technology has reached the stage at which efforts to remedy its own mistakes seem to take us closer to disaster. The vision needed is nothing more than a series of images of physical realities so conceived that one

could hope for an improvement of the human condition." [1]

The projects proposed by Nelson and his class foreshadowed changes soon to come or actually initiated them—but either way, they came to pass. One project by Andy Lee proposed that a multistory garage that occupied Boston's Post Office Square be covered with a park and café, and bordered with shops at street level. In 1990 the garage was demolished and turned into a park by a civic and business partnership with the landscape architects Halvorson Design Partnership. The most significant differences between the actual park and Lee's original proposal were that the garage was placed underground so that the park could rest at street level, and thus no shops were needed to buffer the garage.

This is the aspect of The Hidden City that Nelson miscalculated; he didn't think that governments and businesses would be willing to finance moving entire buildings underground, and so he proposed building pyramidal structures over existing low-rise buildings. He would be pleasantly surprised today; in addition to Post Office Square Park, there have been many examples across the United States of parking lots and even highways being moved underground to make room for green areas on street level, one of the most prominent being Boston's Rose Kennedy Greenway, one component of the city's $22 billion Big Dig.

Over time the fault lines in any good idea begin to show. Concepts lose their strength as they wear or are exaggerated, copied, or transplanted, or as society changes around them, and this is true of each of the projects discussed here.

A few decades of Mobil's copy-paste approach to gas station design has produced widespread homogeneity and killed off incentive for local station owners to build something of their own. Arne Jacobsen's 1936 Skovshoved Gas Station in Copenhagen and Albert Frey's 1965 Tramway Gas Station in Palm Springs are just a couple from a roster of great one-off mid-century stations. However, for every great gas station designed before the standardized approach set in, there were thousands of dismal roadside gas shacks. Noyes's plan for consistency has had its price; over the years the Mobil station designs have been slowly diluted, and though they are generally comfortable places, they are equally mediocre.

The ideas embraced by Design Research have also had problematic repercussions. Variety, the spice of life—introduced to high design by Thompson—has since infiltrated every product sector, to the point where even choosing a beverage from the hundreds available at the market opens paralyzing floodgates of opportunity. A similar onslaught has befallen the furniture business. Rather than focusing on doing a few things well, the brands that attempt to compete with the market barrage produce expansive and incoherent collections and lose their identity. These companies would have consumers refurnishing their homes every six months,

1   GEORGE NELSON, "THE HIDDEN CITY," ARCHITECTURE PLUS, NOVEMBER-DECEMBER (1974), PP. 70–7.

and their designers become pawns in a game of marketing rather than instrumental players in brand vision. Clearly Thompson is not to blame, but his ideas have been poorly extended. Nelson's ideas have also been implemented widely, similarly perhaps with too little discretion at times.

Design is one big conversation between generations. One generation familiarizes itself with the achievements and mistakes of the previous group, hopefully learns something, then tears down some of the mistakes and makes some new claims, leaving a trail of successes and errors for the next generation to discover and react to. Layer after layer, as the sequence continues, the environment is built around us. At its best, we call this process progress. The selection of works by Noyes, Thompson, and Nelson discussed here gives us a clear reading of the zeitgeist surrounding their generation. They valued comfort, clarity, variety, generosity, respect, individuality, community, and space. They weren't afraid of big, bold moves with wide-reaching impact, and as a result their contributions are integrated into everyday reality to the point that we barely notice them. We can thank them for many of the comforts we enjoy, as well as some of the problems we face.

SEQUENCE
INSTIGATIONS: ENGAGING ARCHITECTURE, LANDSCAPE, AND THE CITY, ED MOHSEN MOSTAFAVI, PETER CHRISTENSEN (ZÜRICH: LARS MÜLLER PUBLISHERS, 2012), PP. 76–81
This essay was my first engagement with the Harvard Graduate School of Design, where I have had ongoing involvement since 2012, organizing a conference on design, teaching workshops, and, more recently, using the school's Philip Johnson Thesis House as a conceptual context for the development of the Twill Weave Daybed [P. 130]. The ideas developed in this essay and at the conference on design we organized at the school (Liminal Objects, 2012) helped me come to the idea that industrial design is developed for the dimension between architecture and the human body.

TOP   Design Research Headquarters, Cambridge, Massachusetts, Benjamin Thompson & Associates, Architects, 1969

RIGHT   Service stations for Mobil Oil, Eliot Noyes & Associates, c.1965

LEFT   Proposal for green space and cafés at Boston's Post Office Square, Andy Lee for the GSD class The Hidden City taught by George Nelson, 1973

IMPRESSIONS FROM WALMART

Three floors
Waxy white tiles
Fluorescent ceilings
Baby blue walls
Separate escalators for shopping carts

Electronics & Office
Movies, Music & Books
Home, Furniture & Patio
Apparel, Shoes & Jewelry
Baby & Kids
Toys & Video Games
Sports, Fitness & Outdoors
Auto & Home Improvement
Photo, Gifts, Craft & Party Supplies
Pharmacy, Health & Beauty
Grocery & Pets

Every imaginable extension of the human body
All in a cheap one–stop shop

A teenage girl runs by, excited about something
A blind woman makes her way down the DVD aisle
Old men looking like pirates wait for the elevator

Yarn in primary and pastel colors for $2.77 a spool
Brother 10–Stitch Portable Sewing Machine for $78.88
Striped spandex pants stretched to what could be their limit
Plain Wood Dowel, 5/8" for $1.17

Long black hair hanging over a blue Walmart apron
Zebra Print Bed Rest Pillow, Hot Pink for $6.45
12" Folding Step Stool for $16.94

Everything looks the same

I can't remember which way I came in
I see every type of pot and every type of pan
It's the complete gamut of cooking supplies
But none of them particularly well designed
Or particularly bad either

All the objects at Walmart are in limbo
Between raw material and resting in a landfill
Between a factory and someone's home

Made in China
Made in Taiwan
Made in Vietnam
Made in Mexico

I catch a potent whiff of plastic

X–Factor Neon Orange Duct Tape, $20.82 for a six pack
Black and Decker Piranha Steel 140T Blade, 7.25" for $4.48
Mother and daughter in matching pink sweat suits, Starter
Rust–Oleum Metallic Spray Paint, Aluminum for $3.77

There's a dried–out dusty shop clerk
Forty–something, looking like a vagrant
Smelling like air freshener, restocking sand–paper
I realize that I've never seen anyone move slower

The floor squeaks beneath my sneakers
Squeak, squeak

If the body replaces all of its fat cells every ten years
then how long does it take to sell everything in this store?

Vanilla Scented Candles, $23.97 for a set of three
Legs like tree trunks stemming from white Air Jordans
Warm Apple Pie Scented Candles, $19.97 for a set of four
Flameless LED Tea Lights, no scent, $15.97 for a 36 pack

Passing a woman in a tight aisle there is a shared intimacy
Like we're in a long and narrow room together

A very large woman rolls by
On a Walmart shopping–cart–wheel–chair
Like the humans in the movie WALL–E

Big Joe Bean Bag Chair for $29.00
It has side pockets for magazines
Like the sofa Jasper Morrison did for Cappellini
Except this rendition is terrible

Designers always talk about trickle down
As if it's a good thing

Three friends are in the Outdoors section
Just hanging out, not shopping, only chatting
Surrounded by all this camping equipment

Exerpeutic Fitness Walking Electric Treadmill for $349.00
Gold's Gym 110–lb. Olympic Barbell Weight Set for $98.00
GoFit Yoga Mat with Yoga Position Poster for $15.70
Red Beats headphones on a white Kings baseball hat, shaved head

A strong wind of perfume lingers in the picture frame aisle

A customer service representative is on the phone
"We're out of stock, we do have it, but we're out of stock"
"I'm pretty sure that another Walmart has it"

Another Walmart
A parallel world
There are 4,263 of them in 16 countries
And they average 197,000 square feet per store
Which makes a total of 30 square miles of Walmart
Manhattan is only 23 square miles

Christmas chocolates are on sale

And Valentines Day candies have arrived
Which results in a smooth gradient from red to pink
Running down the candy aisle

Over the intercom
"Attention associates, it is now time for a safety sweep"
"Please walk your areas, safety first"

I got a shopping cart
I was feeling naked in here without one

IMPRESSIONS FROM WALMART
VERITIES, 2013, PP. 99–103
A request from the editors of Verities magazine
to contribute to their third issue, which was devoted
to class, led me to consider the deteriorating legacy
of modern mass-production in industrial design.
What was once an idealistic idea—great design for the
masses—has digressed into the present day situation,
where the vast majority of products transition from
factory to shipping container to mass-retailer to home
to landfill. I had never been to a Walmart before—which
struck me as the epicenter of mass production in today's
world—and so I took the opportunity to record notes
of my impressions. The resulting notes take on the
characteristics of a poem, and though I'm not a poet, I do
consider the format of writing as part of the design of
a text. I approach an essay and the design of an object
or space in largely the same way; there is a thesis, a
subject matter, a material or format, and, finally, the
development of these ideas and forms through
the editing process.

82 Acknowledgements / *Impressum*

Exhibition concept / *Ausstellungskonzept*
Jasper Morrison, Jonathan Olivares & Marco Velardi

Art direction / *Künstlerische Leitung*
SM ASSOCIATI

Vitra Design Museum
Directors / *Direktoren*
Mateo Kries, Marc Zehntner

Exhibition Coordination / *Ausstellungskoordination*
Chrissie Muhr, Jochen Eisenbrand
Public Relations / *Presse- und Öffentlichkeitsarbeit*
Viviane Stappmanns, Denise Beil,
Sabine Müller, Gianoli PR
Visitor services / *Besucherdienst*
Christina Scholten, Anna Deninotti, Annika Schlozer

Source Material explores the references, keepsakes, objects, and books that have informed, provoked, and stimulated a selection of people working in various creative disciplines today.

The three organizers – designers Jasper Morrison, Jonathan Olivares and creative director Marco Velardi – asked a group of sixtytwo creative minds, from the fields of architecture, art, cuisine, design, film, and music, to provide a piece of source material of personal value, found within their regular working or living environment. Seen as points of departure – not ends – from which the creative mind orients itself, these references capture some of the raw impetus, pre-work scratchings of the group of people involved.

Our material world is built up in a succession of layers – generation by generation, work by work – with each new layer informed by and created in dialogue with previous layers.
The spaces we occupy, the food we eat, the books and websites we read and look at, the songs we listen to, the art we spend time with, the films we watch, and the objects we live with.

ial erforscht die Erinnerungsstücke, Kunst- oder
stände und Bücher, die Menschen in verschiedenen
schöpferischer Tätigkeit inspiriert haben und auch
spirieren.

toren der Ausstellung – die Designer Jasper Morrison
Olivares sowie Kreativdirektor Marco Velardi – baten
on 62 Kreativen aus Architektur, Kunst, Kulinarik,
und Musik, Quellenmaterial von persönlichem Wert
iglichen Arbeits- oder Lebensumfeld vorzustellen.
ände sind dabei nicht etwa Schluss-, sondern
kte, an denen sich der kreative Geist orientiert; sie
von den spontanen Impulsen oder auch sorgfältigen
ein, die dem Werk vorausgehen.

Welt um uns herum ist durch eine Sedimentierung
nen und Werken entstanden, bei der jede neue
den Kontakt mit früheren Schichten geprägt oder
wurde. Die Räume, in denen wir uns aufhalten, die
die wir essen, die Bücher und Webseiten, die wir lesen

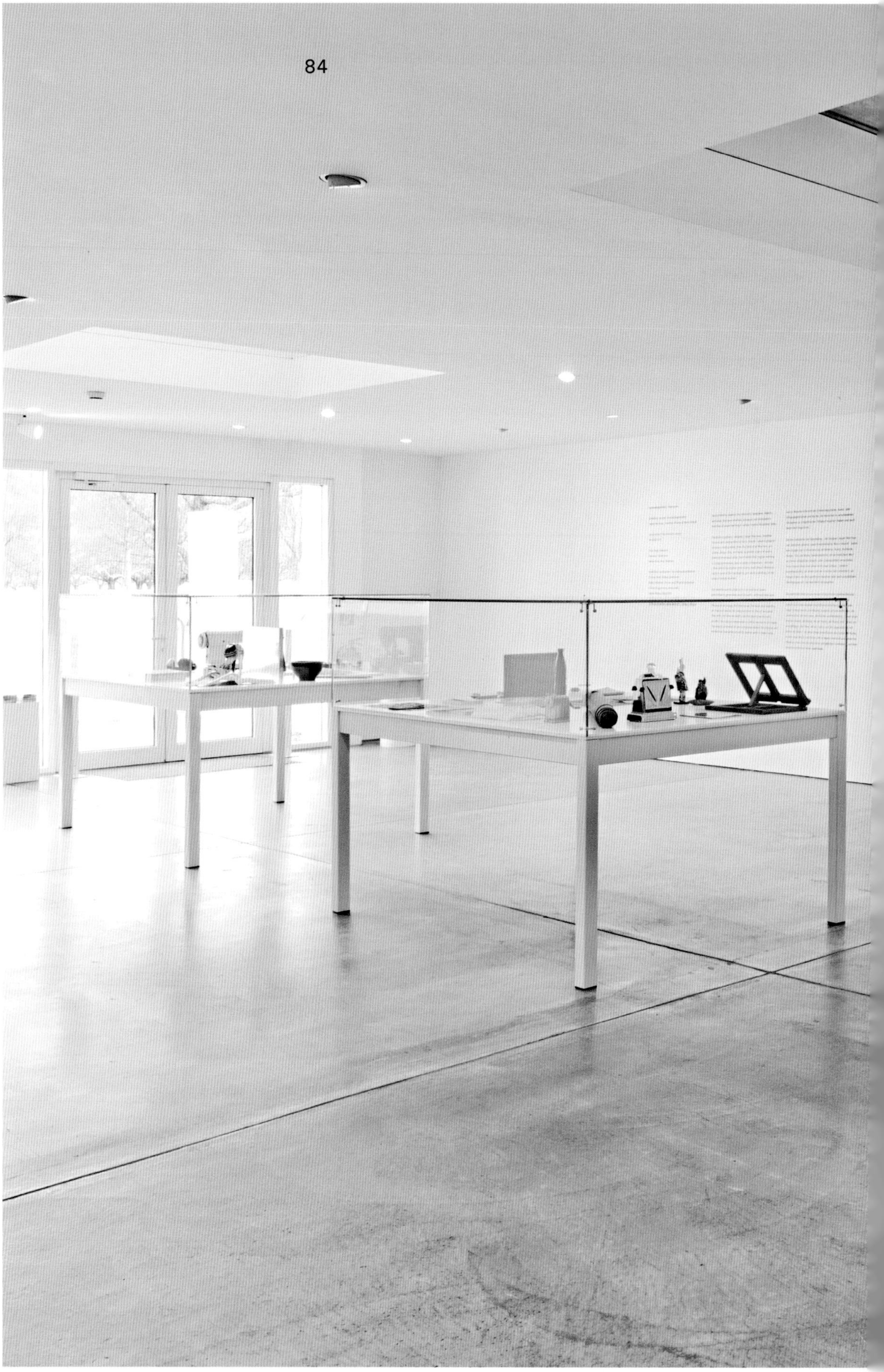

Marco Romanelli   Klaus Hackl

SOURCE MATERIAL
WITH JASPER MORRISON AND MARCO VELARDI,
KALEIDOSCOPE'S PROJECT SPACE, MILAN, APRIL 8,
2014–APRIL 12, 2014, AND VITRA DESIGN MUSEUM, WEIL
AM RHEIN, OCTOBER 24, 2014–APRIL 12, 2014

Jasper Morrison, Marco Velardi, and I hatched the idea for this show over dinner at Jasper's apartment in Paris in the autumn of 2013. We wanted to study how layers of past material culture prompt new layers of material culture, and how the creative mind learns from and leverages an existing object in the creative process. We asked fifty-nine luminaries from the fields of architecture, art, cuisine, design, fashion, film, and music to each contribute an object that had been a stepping stone in the development of their practice. Contributors were also asked to provide a statement about the object they provided describing its origins and what role it has played in their work, and these statements were printed in exhibition pamphlets and the catalog for the show.

We were able to see how the objects were present in the work of their beholders. Some are detected quite literally: a carving tool shows up in the forms of the wooden objects it helps shape; a piece of polished aluminum creates a visual effect that is directly translated to architecture; and stainless-steel props are photographed for a still life. Other objects find their way into their owners' work more subtly: an apron inspires love of honest cooking, workmanship, and family; an old zine "galvanizes" an individual's "passion for supporting creative community"; and a trombone mouthpiece placed inside a trumpet mute–"an element to create loud sounds and an element to stifle them"–reminds its owner to strive for "pleasurable tension."

The exhibition included objects lent to us by K.K. Barret, Frank Benson, Bless, Erwan Bouroullec, Ronan Bouroullec, Laurent Brancowitz, Santi Caleca, Michel Charlot, David Chipperfield, Carter Cleveland, Ilse Crawford, Cecilia Dean, Thomas Demand, Michelle Elie, Frida Escobedo, Eva Franchi, Naoto Fukasawa, Kersten Geers, Zoe Ghertner, Konstantin Grcic, Klaus Hackl, Gabrielle Hamilton, Jaime Hayon, Edwin Heathcote, Fergus Henderson, Sam Hodgekin, Takashi Homma, Frederieke Janssen, Nicholas Lander, Jürg Lehni, Italo Lupi, Michael Maharam, Yves Marbier, Michael Marriott, Mike Meiré, Mike Mills, Pernilla Ohrstedt, Jeffrey Osborne, Sonya Park, Mark Parker, Harsh Patel, Signe Persson Melin, Marco Romanelli, Witold Rybczynski, Richard Sapper, Inga Sempe, Shirana Shabazi, SO–IL, Benjamin Sommerhalder, Andrew Stafford, Massimo Torrigiani, Ramdane Touhami, Jean Touitou, David Van Severen, Justin Vernon, Miguel Viera Baptista, and Wendy Yao–and Jasper, Marco, and I each contributed an object of our own.

SKATEBOARD RAILS

This pair of 1980s skateboard rails, made
from milled nylon, is screwed to the
underside of a skateboard to provide grip for
airs, protect the board's graphic, and allow
the board to slide smoothly on obstacles.
These are some of the first things I can
remember assembling myself, along with the
rest of the skateboard, using a screwdriver.
There was a wonderful sense of fulfillment in
putting a board together.
    Skateboard culture in general left me
with a great sense of workmanship; you
built ramps, assembled decks, learned to
shoot sports photography and edit video,
and sought out the best skate spots by
day and night. Skateboarding was my first
multidisciplinary activity. You would also
adapt things for new uses, inventively.
Handrails, wheelchair ramps, and stairways
became obstacles for any number of tricks,
and the search for these objects throughout
the city of Boston taught me to question
the intended value of a thing, never accepting
its established boundaries.
    Years later, I would remember these
skateboard rails when working on the
stacking bumpers for my Aluminum Chair.
I adapted them to protect the chair from the
abuses of stacking life.

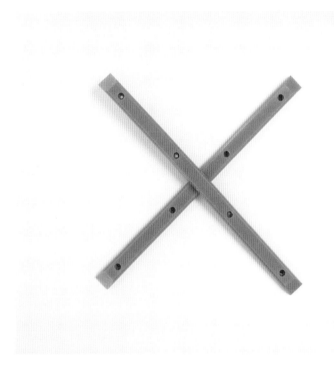

SKATEBOARD RAILS
SOURCE MATERIAL, ED. JASPER MORRISON, JONATHAN
OLIVARES, MARCO VELARDI (MILAN: KALEIDOSCOPE
PRESS, 2014 AND WEIL AM RHEIN: VITRA DESIGN
MUSEUM, 2014)
For the exhibition Source Material [P. 82], Jasper
Morrison, Marco Velardi, and I each contributed an
object that belonged to us. Looking at the objects
that have influenced my work, I decided to include this
pair of skateboard rails, and writing the descriptive text
made me realize the impact that the sport had on my
early formation and outlook on work.

ADAPTATION

Every so often, the way humans go about making things is fundamentally affected by a technological invention. When this happens, it is usually met with some natural resistance by those who are used to and invested in making things the "old way." It usually takes outsiders, the people with nothing to lose and everything to gain, to instigate the process of adapting new technologies towards the production of everyday things.

Craig Ellwood was one of these outsiders, who set out to develop an architecture around the steel frame at a time when the building industry in his city of Los Angeles was rooted in woodworking, one of the oldest construction methods around. If ever there was someone to eschew tradition it was Ellwood. The man renamed himself (he was born Jon Nelson Burke) after a contracting company he helped found, which was itself named after a liquor store; he adopted the title of architect after shedding the title of industrial designer, which he had taken on after working as a building contractor; and eventually he gave up being an architect in Los Angeles to become a painter in Italy. But in the 1950s, Ellwood's focus was on making a name for himself by building architecture with factory-made steel frames and non-load-bearing walls composed of premade panels. And while he wasn't the first to use these technologies in architecture, he implemented them so systematically, repeatedly, and elegantly that he helped adapt them into the visual vocabulary of residential and commercial architecture.

One of the most pointed expressions of Ellwood's pursuits is his Case Study House Number 18, completed in 1958. The house was built under Arts & Architecture magazine's Case Study House program, which sponsored the design and construction of model homes for the postwar US housing boom. Built economically and with the aid of modern techniques, the Case Study Houses helped create a residential architecture that the soldiers returning from World War II could afford.

Ellwood's Case Study House Number 18 teems with economy. The steel framework that supports the house is comprised of 16 x 16 foot (4.9 x 4.9 m) modules that were factory-assembled and then welded together onsite by a team of four men in only eight hours. In a city where most homes were nailed and screwed together out of wood over the course of several months, Ellwood's design offered a radical alternative. The key to the Case Study House Number 18's efficiency is in Ellwood's details: a grid of 2 x 2 inch (5 x 5 cm) columns and 2 x 5.5 inch (5 x 14 cm) beams are outfitted with steel receptors that allow cladding, doors, and window panels to be quickly and easily locked into place. This panel language is where Ellwood's architectural grid gains its human appeal.

The common criticism of architectural grids is that they are too systematic or sterile, but Ellwood populated his industrial steel grid with a lively array of panels that range in function, material, and opacity, and collectively create warm domestic spaces. The panels are made of a restricted palette of simple and widely available materials. Exterior panels are plastic-faced plywood, interior panels are mahogany plywood, window panels are glass or louvered glass, and some of the ceiling panels are blue-wire glass, which softens the sun and filters exterior floodlights into blue light at night. The exterior glass panels are lined from the inside with curtains, and some steel frames extend beyond the house to define outdoor patio areas. Even the fireplace was made as a steel frame, filled with brickwork on account of its flame resistance. All of these elements combine into what appears to be, from photographs, a stunning house.

The diversity of materials, some matte and others reflective, the varied spatial depths achieved by the open and closed structural framework, and the light and shadows that are sculpted by the various textures and depths throughout the building, combine to form a rich spatial composition that blends the house into the surrounding hills and trees. This interplay was something that Ellwood was aware of and handled masterfully: "The infinite delight and richness of decoration can be validly conveyed with rhythmical patterns of texture, mass, line, color, light, and shadow, properly integrated and rendered by machined structure and machine materials."[1] Ellwood's human touch helped prove that machine-made could be as humane as handmade.

The house's grid, as animated as it is, works in large part because of how Ellwood oriented the house to its adjacent landscapes and vistas. To the north, the hills and trees frame the house when seen from the south, and to the south, the view out to the city fills the window frames when looking out from the house. Without the natural vegetation, hills, and views that surround the house, the factory-made rectilinear forms of the Case Study House Number 18 might not feel so kind, as the former softens the latter a great deal.

The project received wide press coverage, and helped bring Ellwood's architecture office a steady stream of commissions. But the building's success was also instrumental in promoting the steel frame technology used to make it, and in forming a new visual language around this technique.

Once such a clear expression of a technology's potential is realized, what follows is predictable: the group of people invested in producing and supporting that technology gain a mascot to help them grow and expand their business, as increasing numbers of conscious emulators and anonymous builders perpetuate the newly realized formal language. And indeed, the steel frame house was the subject of innumerable copies during the subsequent decades, many of which went through the motions of being a steel frame house, albeit without any of the elegance, life, and interplay with the surrounding landscape that embodied the Case Study House Number 18.

Ellwood predicted that rising labor costs would eventually force homes to

1   NEIL JACKSON, CALIFORNIA MODERN: THE ARCHITECTURE OF CRAIG ELLWOOD (NEW YORK: PRINCETON ARCHITECTURAL PRESS, 2002), P. 99.

be made like products in factories, and he wanted to anticipate that future with his buildings. Most of the components of today's homes are made in factories, but they have none of the refinement of Ellwood's components. The average homebuilder in Los Angeles today works with steel studs buried behind walls, low-quality wooden 2 x 4 inch (5 x 10 cm) beams, ubiquitous and drab drywall, and pneumatic nail guns that quicken the assembly process. But efficiency doesn't equate to quality.

Ellwood was an advocate of new technologies, but it was his handling of them that made his buildings so good. Two interesting things to consider about new technologies: they never fully replace the old technologies, but rather become another instrument in the toolbox of available technologies; and as isolated entities, technologies have almost no bearing on the quality or outcome of the buildings or products they help make. Adapting and crafting technology into a quality outcome—today, as in the 1950s—falls upon the Ellwoods of the world.

ADAPTATION
SQM: THE QUANTIFIED HOME, ED. SPACE CAVIAR,
JOSEPH GRIMA, ANDREA BAGNATO, TAMAR SHAFRIR
(ZÜRICH: LARS MÜLLER PUBLISHERS, 2014), PP. 96–101
This text explores Craig Ellwood's Case Study House
Number 18, which revolutionized house construction
with the industrial design of its metal beams, columns,
and non-load-bearing panels. The house achieved
warmth and nuance with its carefully arranged grid
of diverse materials, and Ellwood's approach to wall
construction offered up exactly the kind of craft that
I found missing in the drywall I described in "Today's
Walls" [P. 62]. Learning about Ellwood's wall construction
furthered my interest in the potential of architectural
manufacturing, an interest that took physical form in
the Aluminum Bench [P. 96], which uses a twenty-first
century wall-building technology.

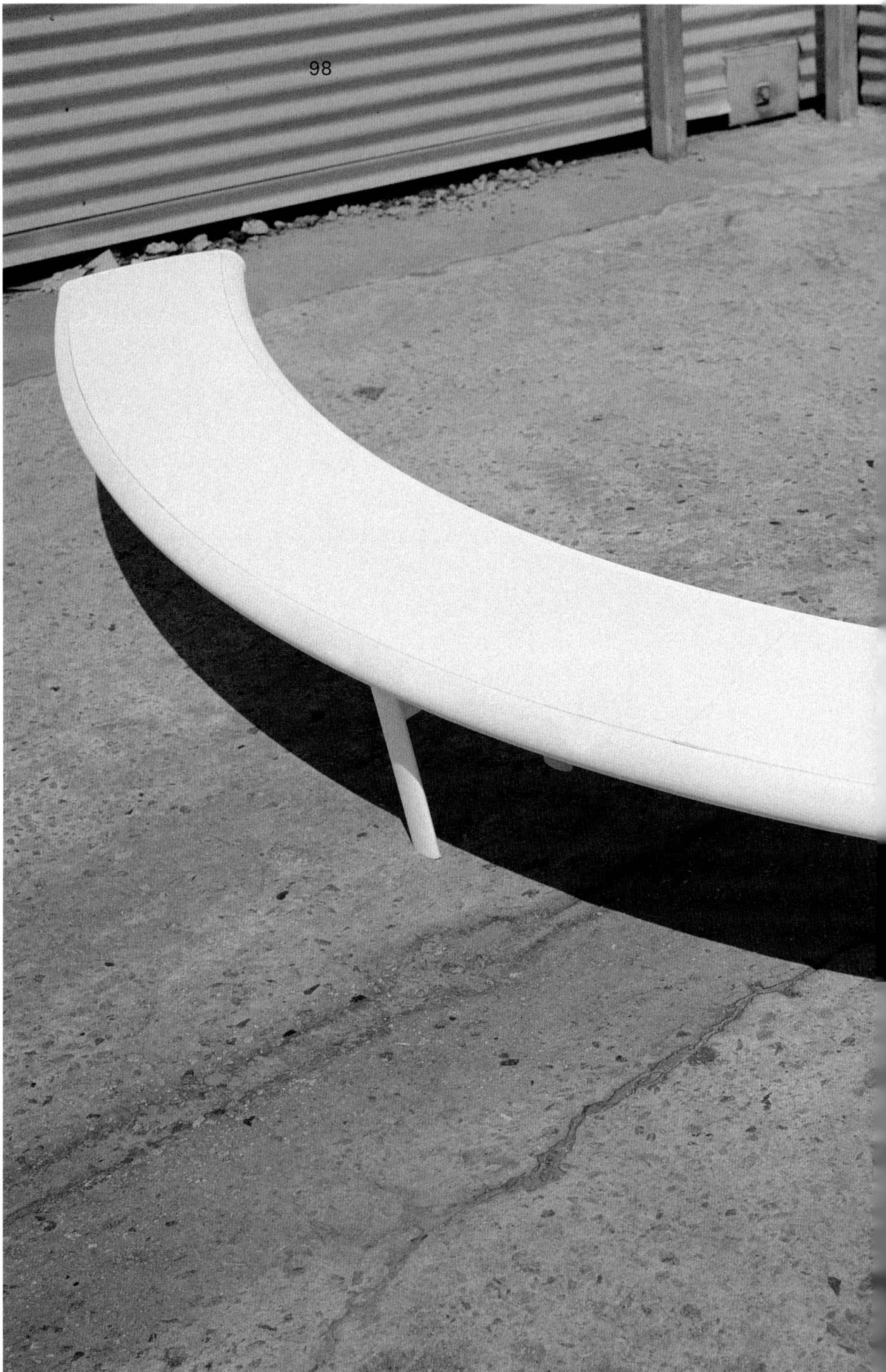

ALUMINUM BENCH
ZAHNER, USA, 2015
Using extrusions and a rolling process which Zahner
had developed for complex curvilinear building
facades, the Aluminum Bench applies architectural
manufacturing processes to the scale of furniture.
The bench was designed for Zahner's web-based
software platform ShopFloor [P. 104], which combines
generative algorithms and 3D software—a combination
that has advanced architectural manufacturing—
and results in a streamlined production of highly
individualized shapes. ShopFloor allows the user to
determine the curvature, length, and color of the bench
for specific architectural contexts. There is a minimum
bend radius of approximately four feet (122 cm), but
beyond that any shape or length bench is possible.

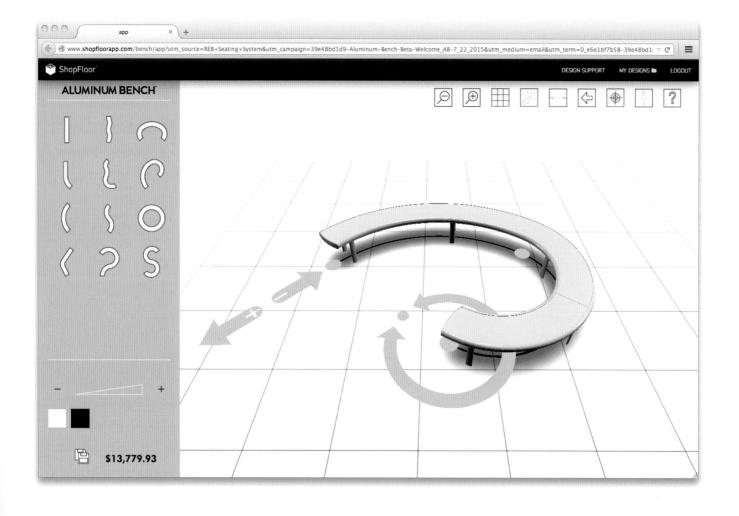

SHOPFLOOR: ALUMINUM BENCH
ZAHNER, USA, 2015
The ShopFloor web tool for the Aluminum Bench [P. 96]
allows the user to choose from a number of predesigned
shapes, scale those shapes, alter them using
manipulation points, or draw entirely new bench shapes.
This web tool also updates the bench price in real time,
and allows each bench design to be sent to Zahner's
engineers. From this file, diagrams and part quantities
are automatically generated for production
on the factory floor.

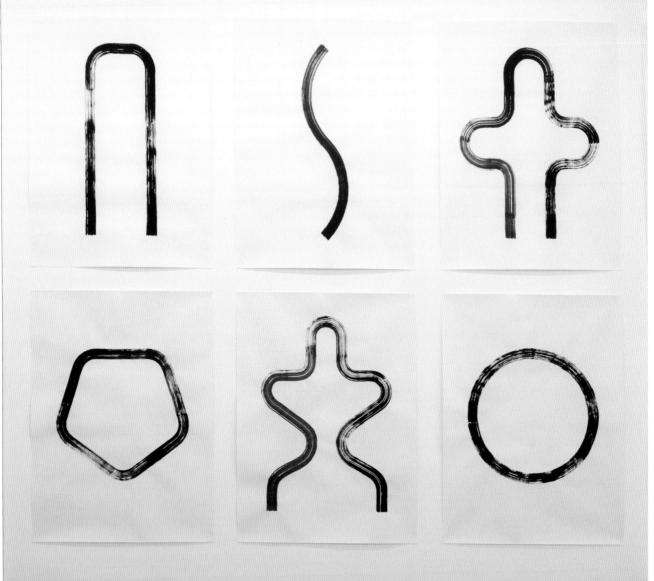

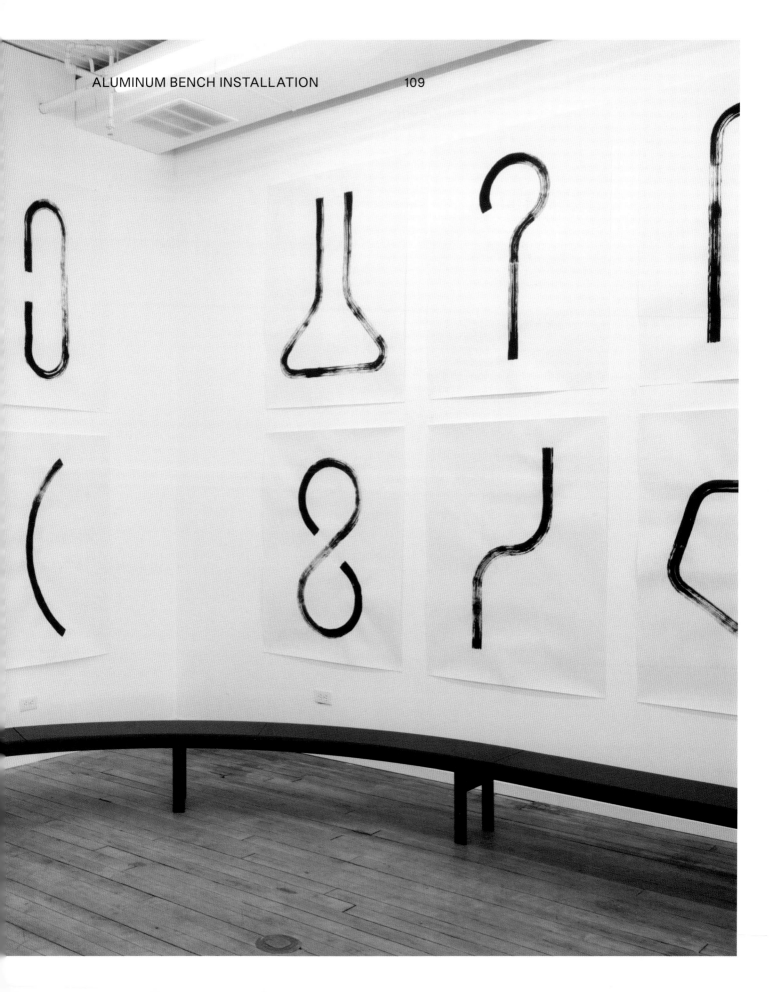

ALUMINUM BENCH INSTALLATION
WITH DRAWINGS BY NATE ANTOLIK, VOLUME GALLERY,
CHICAGO, 2015
For the debut of the Aluminum Bench [P. 96] at Volume
Gallery, I commissioned the artist Nate Antolik to
draw a series of possible bench shapes, based on an
understanding of the limitations of the production
process that makes the bench. The resulting hand-drawn
works were displayed adjacent to the bench, and have
since served as the basis for actual benches.

"I am intrigued by h
can allow for openn
The idea is fascinat
a product, and the
and adds to it, char
beautiful form of su
Hack is such a prod
Konstantin Grcic

Hack
Konstantin Grcic
Available end of 2015

VITRA WORKSPACE
WITH PERNILLA OHRSTEDT, VITRA CAMPUS,
WEIL AM RHEIN, 2015
The Vitra Workspace houses a comprehensive
overview of Vitra's furniture for offices and public
spaces, and is a dynamic planning and learning tool for
these environments. The space occupies the second
floor of a factory building designed by Frank Gehry in
1989, which is located between the Vitra Design Museum,
a factory, the VitraHaus, and the Citizen Office. In location
and in concept, the Workspace is a nexus that connects
intellectual ideas about design with practical office
solutions, and bridges the informality of the home and
public sphere with the demands of the office. Several
installations—including a revolving billboard of life-size
photos of Vitra-furnished offices shot by Daniele Ansidei;
a factory view with scrolling LED text that explains the
processes underway; two seating bars; and a reference
library and a materials library—provoke curiosity and a
deeper understanding of issues in the contemporary
office and of Vitra's unique approach. The space was
designed in collaboration with the architect Pernilla
Ohrstedt and the graphic designer Harsh Patel.

LESSONS FROM THE GIRARD ARCHIVES

Roughly two years ago, while reading an essay that I've since spent hours trying to find without any success, I came across the words "paraphernalia of an active mind." The phrase was used to describe the contents of the protagonist's interior, which was filled with books, models, collected objects, and tools. The protagonist was a genius in his field, surrounded himself with these objects and evidently used them as stepping-stones for his own working process. The idea that an active mind benefits, from and perhaps depends on, tangible accessories is not new, but phrased in this way I found it so compelling that it stayed with me long after I had forgotten the source.

More recently, I was asked by the editors of this catalog to contemplate the legacy of Alexander Girard's design practice within the field of contemporary design. On first consideration, the request pointed toward an analysis of devices found in the Girard toolshed: the use of vivid pattern and color in furniture and textiles, and the transfer of knowledge from indigenous craft processes to modern product and branding efforts. These methods are interesting in that they represent a specific approach to design, but I hoped to find and explore the most versatile apparatus within Girard's repertoire of tools. Having had some exposure to Girard's taxonomic collection of folk art, which he acquired during his global travels, I saw the opportunity to explore the ample notion of Girard's very own paraphernalia: what it was, where and why he collected it, how he organized it, how it empowered his design process, and what might be learned from this activity. Paraphernalia, references, source material–whatever name it goes by–is always specific to the mind that gathers and uses it, which is to say that it can aid the development of an endless variety of interests and approaches.

Collections of source material have abounded in the workplaces of many celebrated minds from many different disciplines. For the film Eyes Wide Shut the film director and producer Stanley Kubrick commissioned some thirty thousand photographs of doorways, gates, coffee shops, costume shops, hospitals, bedrooms, toy shops, and mortuaries. These helped him select locations and reproduce real life scenarios that might have never occurred to a production designer. Between 1948 and 1973, the artist Ellsworth Kelly built a collection of visual references comprised of sketches and cutouts from envelopes, magazines, maps, menus, newspapers, and packaging. Kelly later assembled these items onto tablets, which are considered art works. Today the tablets are housed at the Menil Foundation in Houston, and the artist continues to return to them when making new works.

For the 2014 exhibition Source Material, which I organized with Jasper Morrison and Marco Velardi, we called upon over sixty individuals from the fields of art, architecture, cooking, graphic design, industrial design, fashion, production design, and music to provide us with a single object that had informed or provoked their own creative process. With some light prodding, everyone we asked was able to come up with an object and write a cogent paragraph about how that object had elevated their work. The architect Frida Escobedo gave us a piece of petrified wood, which was a catalyst for her approach to architecture: "Patterns found in materials such as wood or certain types of stone are informed by their own formation and the conditions under which this process took place. In a similar fashion, the architectural object develops via deposition and erosion, by inhabitation, appropriation, exchange, and agency. In that sense, if form follows function, it was crucial for me to understand that function is never static, definite, or predictable."[1] That she was able to extract all of this from a piece of old wood is a testament to the power of an object to carry metaphors, trigger associations, and augment the creative process.

Alexander Girard began collecting folk art in 1939 while he and his wife Susan were on their honeymoon in Mexico, and while he gathered an abundant and diverse array of references over the course of his career, his collection retains a high degree of focus. In his introduction to The Magic of People: Folk Art and Toys from the Collection of the Girard Foundation, Girard states the rationale behind his collecting activity: "We can, and I firmly believe we should, preserve evidence of the past, not as a pattern for sentimental imitation, but as nourishment for the creative spirit of the present, so that we too may evolve customs and shape objects of equivalent value in our own way, in our own time, taking advantage of the many new methods and materials at our disposal."[2] While Girard's collection is centered on folk and indigenous art, the breadth he achieved within this framework is formidable.

One index for Girard's archive includes some of the following categories: Adam and Eve, artificial leaves, airplanes, antique plaster, balancing toys, balls, banks, bird cages, buildings, butterflies, calico dolls, candy containers, charro buttons, Christmas ornaments, churches, circuses and acrobats, crosses, cut-outs, devils, die-cut paper, dog toys, doll houses, edible figures, Ferris wheels, fertility symbols, flowers, fold-outs, found objects, furniture, games, graphics, hats and headdresses, hotel stationery, juvenile drama, kachinas (dolls used to represent supernatural beings in the Hopi religion), kites, labels, lead, masks, matches, marbles, merry-go-rounds, mini fruit, mini insects and birds, Muslim prints, music boxes, musical instruments, musicians, Nativity, new year prints, old coins, paintings, paper dolls, pictures, pre-Columbian, props, puppets, puzzles, religious, ribbons, rocking horses, Santa Claus, shadow theatre, ships, stamps, sugar cubes, teddy bears, textiles, tops, trains, vendors, votives, wedding parties, yarn pictures, yoyo, and cup and ball.

1   FRIDA ESCOBEDO, "PETRIFIED WOOD," SOURCE MATERIAL (MILAN: KALEIDOSCOPE PRESS, 2014, WEIL AM RHEIN: VITRA DESIGN MUSEUM, 2014), P. 36.

2   ALEXANDER GIRARD, THE MAGIC OF A PEOPLE: FOLK ART AND TOYS FROM THE COLLECTION OF THE GIRARD FOUNDATION (NEW YORK: VIKING PRESS, 1968), P. 9.

A closer look into the matchbox section, which is further categorized by location, reveals the geographical diversity of Girard's collection: Arizona, Belgium, California, Chicago, China, Czechoslovakia, England, Estonia, Ethiopia, Finland, France, Ghana, India, Italy, Israel, Japan, Latvia, Mexico, Morocco, New Mexico, Poland, Portugal, Spain, Sweden, Switzerland, USSR, and Yugoslavia. Girard's archives also include over a thousand photographs that he took of cemeteries, markets, and vernacular graphics, and Girard also collaborated with Charles Eames on photography and films that document objects and scenes that were of shared interest.

For every object that Girard chose to include in his collection, there are certainly untold quantities of objects that didn't make the cut. Building a collection is largely an editorial process made up of yes/no operations, and so is the design process. Girard's perpetual collecting would have strengthened his yes/no abilities. Even the neat organization of this material appears to have been a creative procedure in itself. Girard stored all of the samples by category in wooden or cardboard boxes, and the original labeling system—a series of handwritten stickers—is still in use at the Vitra Design Museum today. All of this serves as evidence of the uncountable hours that Girard spent organizing and learning from his stockpile.

One doesn't have to look through Girard's archives for long before spotting some obvious connections between the objects he collected and the spaces and products he designed. While Girard donated part of his collection to the Museum of International Folk Art, Santa Fe (MoIFA), between 1979 and 1981, and another part was given to the Vitra Design Museum after his death in 1993, it is not known exactly when he acquired each of the objects in the collection. What results is a fair amount of uncertainty about the exact relationship between Girard's collection and his design output, as well as a strong sense of the association and codependence between the two bodies of material.

A toy wooden table that Girard purchased in Japan has a hexagonal shape made up of a grid of triangles that resembles Girard's own 1967 Hexagonal Table, made of polished die-cast aluminum. Girard also used a triangular grid of beams as handrails at his 1966 L'Etoile restaurant at the Sherry-Netherland hotel in New York City. A petroglyph of a curled snake that was photographed by Charles Eames on a trip that he and Girard took to La Cienega, Arizona, in 1954 served as the basis for a printed pillow designed by Girard in 1961. His brightly colored and patterned collection of textiles includes samples that he designed and found, and the differences between the two can easily evade the untrained eye. The color palette of pink, orange, pale blue, avocado green, and magenta—which Girard used on the menu of his 1960 La Fonda Del Sol restaurant—appear in similar combinations in the painted wooden planes and clay figurines that Girard purchased in Mexico. Mentorship is a crucial component in the passage of knowledge between humans, so it seems natural that objects can carry knowledge and offer mentorship between craftsmen who never knew each other.

If Girard could be accused of stealing then he falls into a legacy of great thieves. One of director Jim Jarmusch's "Golden Rules of Film Making" states: "Nothing is original. Steal from anywhere that resonates with inspiration or fuels your imagination . . . Select only things to steal from that speak directly to your soul. If you do this, your work (and theft) will be authentic."[3] The poet, critic, and editor T. S. Eliot once stated, "Immature poets imitate; mature poets steal; bad poets deface what they take, and good poets make it into something better, or at least something different."[4] While creative theft is common among today's designers, Girard's particular blend of thievery is unique in that he drew from such a wide and thoroughly researched body of collected artifacts, and he valued the connections between the objects as much as the objects themselves.

Girard's collection of artifacts also made its way directly into the spaces he designed. The La Fonda del Sol restaurant's vibrant interior featured Mexican folk art in vitrines and Mexican ceramic tableware. The 1957 Miller House, designed by Eero Saarinen and furnished by Girard, juxtaposes newly designed and indigenous objects to their mutual benefit. The vibration between past and present objects was a crucial ingredient in Girard's spirited atmospheres.

In an interview with Charlene Cerny, Curatorial Coordinator of the inaugural exhibit in the Girard Wing at MoIFA, Girard states: "Part of my passion has always been to see objects in context. As a collector who was often able to see the actual environment in which a piece was made, I've often felt that objects lose half their lives when they are taken out of their natural settings."[5] Never one to view objects in isolation, Girard took to collecting large quantities of related objects, and when he exhibited these objects he would display them in elaborate scenes that helped establish their context.

In the displays he designed for his own collection at MoIFA a Hopi kachina doll was placed within a village of kachina dolls, architectural backgrounds, painted clay bowls, a wooden snake, and additional Hopi trappings. The kachina dolls, created to represent supernatural beings, were given to children and used to convey parables. One kachina teaches the pollination of corn plants, another encourages children to help with harvesting, and another whips villagers who don't clean communal areas. Understood collectively, the kachina offer a

3   JIM JARMUSCH, "JIM JARMUSCH'S GOLDEN RULES," MOVIEMAKER: THE ART AND BUSINESS OF MAKING MOVIES, 53 (JANUARY 2004): www.MOVIEMAKER.COM/ARCHIVES/MOVIEMAKING/DIRECTING/JIM–JARMUSCH–5–GOLDEN–RULES–OF–MOVIEMAKING.

4   T. S. ELIOT, "PHILIP MASSINGER," THE SACRED WOOD: ESSAYS ON POETRY AND CRITICISM (LONDON: FABER AND FABER, 1920), P. 20.

5   "CHARLENE CERNY IN CONVERSATION WITH ALEXANDER GIRARD," THE MUSEUM OF INTERNATIONAL FOLK, 1979–82, www.INTERNATIONALFOLKART.ORG/EVENTSEDU/EDUCATION/GIRARD/CONVERSATION/WITH/ALEXANDER/GIRARD.PDF.

map of Hopi societal fabric. Girard's dynamic displays of artifacts rekindled the networks of symbolism that were vital to the cultures he collected from.

The interplay of Girard's collecting activity and his design practice provides today's designer with a number of vital lessons:

1 – It offers a singular reaffirmation that a body of references can act as a springboard for new design endeavors.

2 – It shows that preservation of the past is not necessarily nostalgic or antithetical to the conception of new work.

3 – It underscores that the process of building and refining a collection and the process of designing are both editorial in nature.

4 – It demonstrates how old objects and new objects can sit side by side, with the old affording the new a rich legacy of form and the new reinvigorating the old.

5 – It shows that at their best, objects are socially bound to other objects and embedded within social context and cultural practices.

In a time like ours—when design often takes place in the vacuum of a computer screen and the most groundbreaking products often make many existing objects obsolete—we need to absorb Girard's lessons, as much to connect us with our receding past as to inform our precarious future.

LESSONS FROM THE GIRARD ARCHIVES
ALEXANDER GIRARD: A DESIGNER'S UNIVERSE, ED.
MATEO KRIES, JOCHEN EISENBRAND (WEIL AM RHEIN:
VITRA DESIGN MUSEUM, 2016), PP. 320–27
This text provided the opportunity to further the
research that Jasper Morrison, Marco Velardi, and I had
done in Source Material [P. 82], by looking at Alexander
Girard's vast collection of personal references and
studying what role these objects played in his own
design process. This research also gave me the
opportunity to study the textiles that Girard collected,
and how they influenced his own textile designs, just
as I was beginning to design a textile of my own for
the Twill Weave Daybed [P. 130]. What I discovered is
that, like many of the best artists and designers that
came before and after him, Girard was a deft burglar
of good ideas.

REPEAT

"Pete and Repeat were sitting on a fence.
Pete fell off. Who was left? Repeat. Pete and
Repeat were sitting on a fence. Pete fell off.
Who was left? Repeat. Pete and Repeat were
sitting on a fence. Pete fell off. Who was left?
Repeat . . ."
– Bruce Nauman, Raw Materials (2004)

I recently came across this text by
the artist Bruce Nauman while researching
textiles. The words are based on
an old children's joke, and through verbal
repetition Nauman builds a lexical fabric
that emphasizes and expands the meaning
of the words. I was struck by the similarity
between lingual repetition and the kind
of repetition found in textiles, where woven
patterns create larger swaths of cloth.

In a plain weave–the oldest, most
common weave–the warp (the longitudinal
yarn) is crisscrossed by the weft (the yarn
woven between): over, under, over,
under, over, under. The outcome is grid-like
in appearance. In a twill weave, each weft
floats over one or more warp threads before
crossing back under one or more warp
threads: over, over, under, under, over, over,
under, under, over, over, under, under. The
outcome is a diagonal pattern.

Modern textile manufacturing was
born in 1801 with the first demonstration
of the Jacquard loom in Paris. The loom's
binary card was a precursor to digital
computation and storage. Each hole in
these cards dictates whether a Bolus hook
is engaged, which in turn dictates whether
the warp falls above or below the weft.
The card stores a pattern, thus making textile
production repeatable and industrial. The
holes give specific binary input–1,0,1,0,1,0,
which translates to over, under, over, under,
over, under–and this input is illustrated
in the interplay of warp and weft.
The resulting textile is thus a depository
of information and structure; in a sense,
it wears what it stores.

Over time, textile patterns take on
cultural meaning. For instance, in the West,
the plain weave with a visible checker
pattern was used on the arms of de Warenne,
Earl of Surrey, during the medieval period;
some four hundred years later, during
the settlement of the American Midwest,
the pattern reappeared on horse racing flags
(and subsequently became the finish line flag
for modern car racing); in the mid–twentieth
century, designer Alexander Girard used
the checker pattern on furniture; and in
the 1980s, skateboarders began donning the
pattern on their checkered Vans. In each
case, a new layer of cultural meaning is
stored in the textile.

In her book Weaving the Word: The
Metaphorics of Weaving and Female Textual
Production, Kathryn Sullivan Kruger links
ancient textile production, textuality, and
gender: "By participating in the production
of textiles . . . women took part in the first
textual practices, recording their society's
stories, myths, and sacred beliefs in symbols
woven or embroidered on their textiles. The
scene they conveyed constituted society's
first texts." Text is embedded in textile; and
textile is text.

As composed, woven memory, textile is both ornament and shroud, and its functional characteristics are programmed into it. Twill weaves, for instance, are known for their resilient, durable, and cleanable structures, which are also resistant to wrinkling. For this reason, twill is the pattern of choice for denim, curtains, and neckties.

Beyond geometry and structure, materiality is also programmed into a woven textile via the yarn or fiber that is used. It is possible to make yarn in just about any material imaginable—wool, carbon, even steel—and such variation makes textile a highly dynamic and adaptable manufacturing method. Combined with a textiles weave, materials alter the language and structure of a textile, and each material also comes with its own cultural history. Wool, for instance, dates back to the first breeding of wooly sheep some eight thousand years ago in Iran, and the earliest known use of wool textile in Europe is traced to a Danish bog dated to 1500 BC.

Returning to Nauman's title, Raw Materials, I realize that he not only uses individual words as raw material but also larger patterns of words. This is how Nauman is able to turn a children's joke into an artwork; and this is also how one culture can appropriate the same textile pattern as another, but for entirely different ends. Warp and weft are both words and grammar, and together construct durable yet contingent memory systems. Textiles are structures made of binary and linguistic information, material properties, and cultural histories, yet they remain open and allow us to build additional structures such as garments, furnishings, architecture and further cultural histories.

REPEAT
HARVARD DESIGN MAGAZINE,
FALL/WINTER 2016, PP. 144–45
In past writing projects, the themes I have explored
have been tangentially linked to my design projects.
This essay represents something of a breakthrough in
my approach to writing, where the subject came directly
from a design project that I was actively working on.
The text was drafted as I was conceiving the Twill Weave
Textile [P. 128], and writing it gave me the opportunity
to sort out and expand all the references that I had
gathered as I designed the textile.

TWILL WEAVE TEXTILE
KVADRAT, DENMARK, 2016
The construction of this textile was informed by
the twill weave and color of carbon fiber cloth. Carbon
fiber is used in the construction of lightweight and
strong components within the automotive, sailing, and
sporting industries. The development of a sister textile
in wool allows designers to pair the rigid or flexible
components of carbon fiber with a soft upholstered
component, resulting in a total object made entirely
from twill weave cloth. The textile was first used on
the Twill Weave Daybed [P. 130], and will be introduced
in a broader range of colors that—like carbon fiber
itself—come from the earth's crust.

TWILL WEAVE DAYBED
KVADRAT, DENMARK AND HALL COMPOSITES,
USA, 2016
The Twill Weave Daybed, developed with the Danish
textile manufacturer Kvadrat and the New England
manufacturer of sailing masts Hall Composites, is
made predominantly from woven textile. The daybed's
legs and two millimeter-thick flexible resting surface
are manufactured with a twill weave carbon fiber
that is 63 percent cloth by weight, with the remaining
weight comprised of epoxy. The legs and crossbeams
of the daybed are formed with mandrels used by Hall
Composites in the mast-making process, and a matte
finish was developed that emphasizes the woven pattern
of the textile over the epoxy that binds it. With Kvadrat, I
developed a sister textile to the carbon fiber that is made
of wool and is used to upholster the daybed's cushion. As
a result, the entire visible and tactile experience of the
daybed is defined by a continuous, dark gray, twill textile,
which lends warmth and texture to the space around it.
This object tests our ability to engineer woven materials
to diverse effects, and it provides a new aesthetic model
for furniture in which materials can be structurally
diverse yet visually homogenous.

Room for a
Daybed

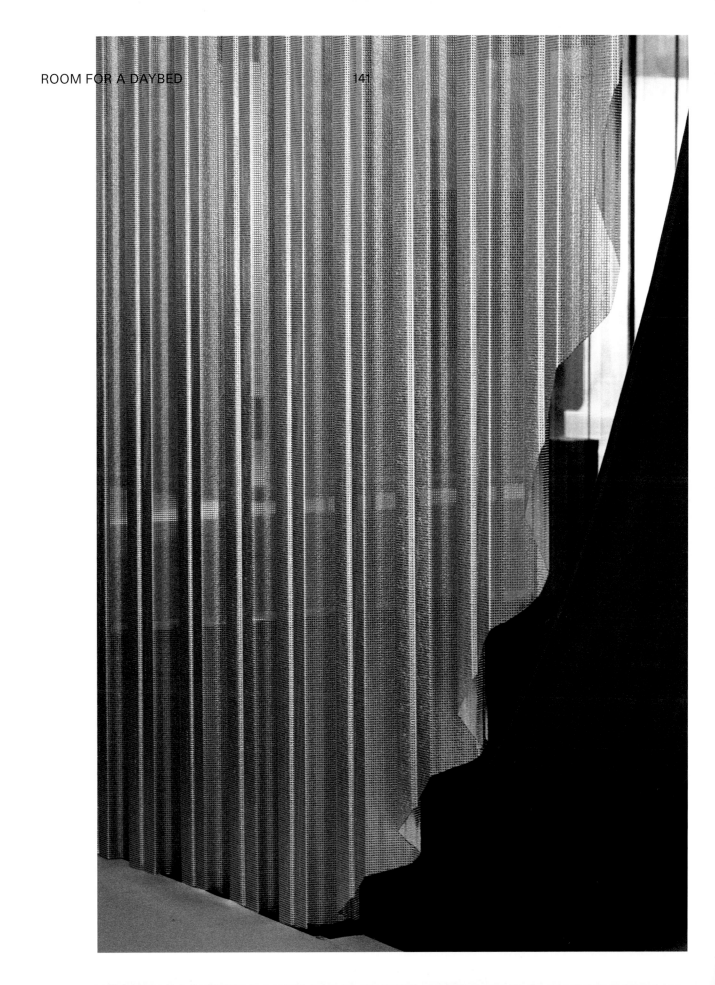

ROOM FOR A DAYBED
WITH JOHNSTON MARKLEE, BIENNAL INTERIEUR,
KORTRIJK, OCTOBER 14, 2016–OCTOBER 23, 2016
Realized in collaboration with the architecture firm
Johnston Marklee, Room for a Daybed represents a
reversal in the typical relationship between architecture
and furniture. Conventionally, furniture is selected or
developed in response to an existing or new building.
With Room for a Daybed we have done the opposite,
developing an interior as a spatial response to the
single object it contains: the Twill Weave Daybed. Like
the daybed, the interior is built of textile, and it seeks
to define a soft architecture. While the daybed draws
from mast construction, the room conceived around
it references sail design. Four inner walls, made from
suspended billowing non-woven textile, occupy much of
the room's volume and create an intimate area around
the daybed. The nested space is oriented at a 45° angle
to the enclosing corrugated steel walls, and has four
entry points at its corners. The floor is covered with a
thick, sound-dampening felt, and the ceiling is open to
the space above. The overhead aperture hosts a single
light source, a lighting balloon used on film and television
sets, that casts daylight temperature light on the
curved walls and daybed below. The space is intended
for contemplation and rest, and explores the wide
structural, spatial, and visual limits of textile.

This project was commissioned by OFFICE Kersten
Geers David Van Severen, Richard Venlet, and Joris
Kritis, and realized with the support of Kvadrat, Hall
Composites, Knoll, and FilzFelt.

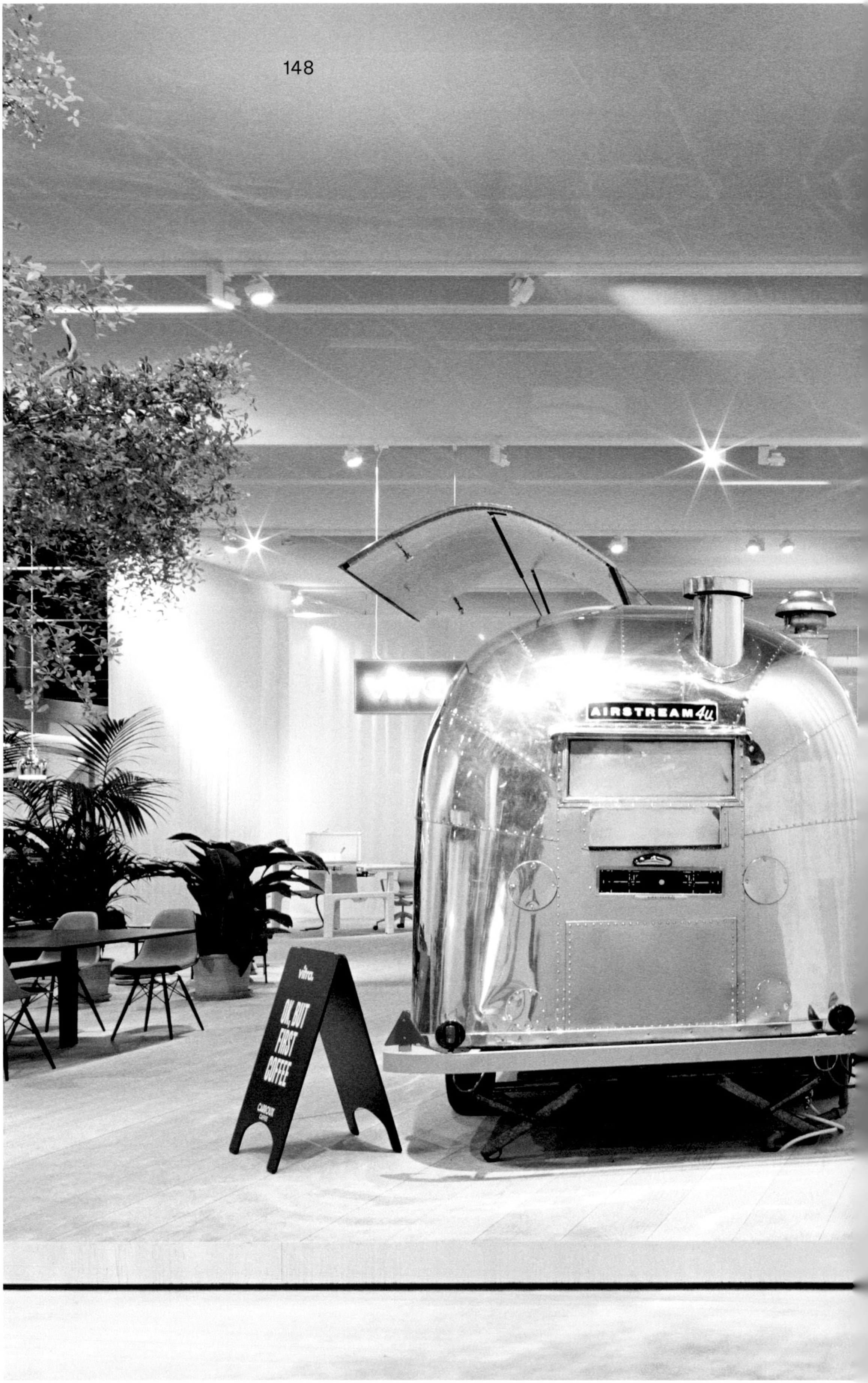
AIRSTREAM 4u
OK, BUT FIRST COFFEE

WORK
WITH PERNILLA OHRSTEDT, VITRA PRESENTATION AT
ORGATEC, COLOGNE, OCTOBER 25, 2016–OCTOBER 29,
2016
Vitra Presents Work is a new hall initiated by Vitra,
occupied with fifteen partner companies—including
purveyors of kitchens, flooring, textiles, wall paneling,
and workplace technologies—and presented at Orgatec in
2016. Pernilla Ohrstedt and I conceived a master plan
and fair concept, imagining the hall as a village of diverse
companies united by the high quality of their products
and their common interest in the future of the office.
The companies are organized around a shared main street
and against a continuous backdrop depicting the earth's
horizon from dawn until dusk.

LIST OF WORKS

SOURCE MATERIAL, First Edition, with Jasper Morrison, Marco Velardi (Milan: Kaleidoscope Press, 2014) – BOOK

SKATEBOARD RAILS, SOURCE MATERIAL, with Jasper Morrison, Marco Velardi, Kaleidoscope Project Space, Milan, 2014 and Vitra Design Museum, Weil am Rhein, 2014 – EXHIBITION

A VIEW ON NATURAL MOTION, with Harsh Patel, www.naturalmotion.nikeinc.com, Nike, 2014 – WEBSITE

KONSTANTIN GRCIC, Konstantin Grcic: Panorama, ed. Mateo Kries, Janna Lipsky (Weil am Rhein: Vitra Design Museum, 2014), PP. 189–95 – ESSAY

VIEW–MASTER, with Harsh Patel, www.jonathanolivares.com/viewmaster, 2014 – WEBSITE

ADAPTATION, SQM: The Quantified Home, ed. Space Caviar (Joseph Grima, Andrea Bagnato, Tamar Shafrif), (Zürich: Lars Müller Publishers, 2014), PP. 96–101 – ESSAY

ALUMINUM BENCH, Domus, November, 2014, PP. 30–32 – ESSAY

SOURCE MATERIAL, with Jasper Morrison, Marco Velardi, Vitra Design Museum, Weil am Rhein, October 24, 2014 / February 8, 2015 – EXHIBITION

SOURCE MATERIAL, Second Edition, with Jasper Morrison, Marco Velardi (Weil am Rhein: Vitra Design Museum, 2015) – BOOK

ALUMINUM BENCH, Zahner, USA, 2015 – FURNITURE

ALUMINUM BENCH, with drawings by Nate Antolik, Volume Gallery, Chicago, June 15, 2015 / July 16, 2015 – EXHIBITION

SHOPFLOOR: ALUMINUM BENCH, with Andrew Manto, Paul Martin, www.shopfloorapp.com/bench/app, Zahner, 2015 – WEBSITE

VITRA WORKSPACE, with Pernilla Ohrstedt, Vitra Campus, Weil am Rhein, 2015 – INTERIOR

JOINTS, Dirty Furniture, September, 2015, PP. 110–23 – ESSAY

LESSONS FROM THE GIRARD ARCHIVES, Alexander Girard: A Designer's Universe, ed. Mateo Kries, Jochen Eisenbrand (Weil am Rhein: Vitra Design Museum, 2016), PP. 320–27 – ESSAY

RICHARD SAPPER EDITED BY JONATHAN OLIVARES, with photography by Ramak Fazel (London: Phaidon Press, 2016) – BOOK

TWILL WEAVE TEXTILE, Kvadrat, Denmark, 2016 – TEXTILE

TWILL WEAVE DAYBED, Kvadrat, Denmark and Hall Composites, USA, 2016 – FURNITURE

ROOM FOR A DAYBED, with Johnston Marklee,
Biennale Interieur, Kortrijk, October 14, 2016 /
October 23, 2016 — EXHIBITION
WORK, with Pernilla Ohrstedt, Orgatec,
Cologne, October 25, 2016 / October 29, 2016
— EXHIBITION

WORKSPIRIT 14, ed. with Pernilla Ohrstedt
(Birsfelden: Vitra, 2016) — PUBLICATION

AN OFFICE PERSPECTIVE, Edited with
Pernilla Ohrstedt (Birsfelden: Vitra, 2016)
— PUBLICATION

REPEAT, Harvard Design Magazine, Fall/
Winter, 2017, PP. 144—45 — ESSAY